DIGITALLY
REMASTERED

A BIBLICAL GUIDE TO
RECLAIMING YOUR
VIRTUAL SELF

D1340488

GUY BRANDON

Muddy
Pearl

First published in 2016 by
Muddy Pearl, Edinburgh, Scotland.
www.muddypearl.com
books@muddypearl.com

© Jubilee Centre 2016

Guy Brandon has asserted his right under the Copyright, Designs and
Patents Act, 1988 to be identified as the author of this work.

All rights reserved. No part of this publication may be reproduced or
transmitted in any form or by any means, electronic or mechanical,
including photocopy, recording, or information storage and retrieval system,
without permission in writing from the publisher. The only exception is brief
quotations in printed reviews or articles.

Unless otherwise indicated, Scripture quotations are taken from
the Holy Bible, New International Version Anglicised,
copyright © 1979, 1984, 2011 Biblica, formerly International Bible Society.
Used by Permission of Hodder & Stoughton Publishers,
an Hachette UK company.
All rights reserved.
NIV is a registered trademark of Biblica.
UK trademark number 1448790.

British Library Cataloguing in Publication Data
A catalogue record for this book is available from the British Library

ISBN 978-1-910012376

Typeset in Minion by Waverley Typesetters, Warham, Norfolk
Printed in Great Britain by Bell & Bain Ltd, Glasgow

For Jennie, Sophie and Joe

ACKNOWLEDGEMENTS

A number of people and organisations have helped this book to see the light of day. The Jubilee Centre's many years of research have provided much of the thinking that underpins the biblical approach to modern communications technologies, and past and present staff have offered much encouragement and feedback over the last two years. David Pullinger's comments on an early article prompted the broader exploration that evolved into the book, and his feedback on a later draft was invaluable. The Cambridge Papers writing group likewise helped to hone and clarify some of the key thinking. Lastly, I'm grateful to Stephanie Heald and Muddy Pearl for showing interest in the original concept and providing assistance and editorial help throughout.

CONTENTS

FOREWORD

In the hours and days following the results of the UK referendum on whether we should leave or remain in the European Union, I took a 48-hour emergency retreat from social media. It had all become a little too much. I found myself obsessed with the analysis, being drawn into the online debate taking place on Twitter and Facebook. I was alarmed at how quickly we separated into two distinct camps – 'the Brexiters' and 'the Remainers'. The amount of vitriol hurled from one side to the other in the frenzied days following the vote to leave was discombobulating. Real life – hopes and dreams and political views and disappointments and despair – had broken into the world of social media. I realised that for many of us, our social media accounts are well-crafted portrayals of how we want our lives to be seen. As well as putting forward our personal brands, we surround ourselves on social media with people who are like us and follow accounts that confirm our worldview. Part of the reason for the hysteria that ensued was that for many, that well-crafted world we had created for ourselves online had all come crumbling down in those few days. Or at least it felt like it. It felt like it because for many people – particularly my generation, the millennials – our whole world can be contained in the social media cocoon. When real life and the real world contradict the cosy digital cocoon we have nestled ourselves in, we start to ask questions about who we are, who our neighbours are and what kind of world we want to live in.

But it's not all bad. My Facebook timeline is often filled with videos of cats and 'Carpool Karaoke' – the facile things of this world that just make us smile. But at times through Facebook or

Twitter, I have reconnected with long-forgotten friends when I have seen from their statuses that they are facing life's difficulties – depression, divorce, death. I have had in-depth conversations about life, love and faith using the Messenger app. I can think of countless times in which I have been so grateful for these new technologies in helping me to make a difference #IRL (in real life).

The web, our smartphones and social media have immense power on our lives. I am, sadly, one of the 80 per cent of smartphone users for whom the very first action in the day is to reach for my phone. It contains my diary, health and fitness apps, my Bible and all my conversations with friends and loved ones over the years. I consult my phone when I want to know what's happened in the world overnight, how to get somewhere, when to leave home to catch the bus or whether I need an umbrella. It provides me with podcasts and my 'pray-as-you-go' app.

Is it any wonder that these technologies have become so entwined with our lives? They have become an extension of ourselves. They can confirm our worldviews or shatter our delusions about the communities in which we live and what it is to be human. They reduce the world to 140 characters, and paint a picture – with appropriate filters and all – of a distorted reality. Can true connection with others – our husbands, wives, families, friends, neighbours and church communities – be truly authentic if it exists only in our computers and smartphones?

What is the Christian response to these technologies that very quickly have become so much a part of our daily lives that online and social media fasts are now required to gain headspace and maintain some sense of sanity? What wisdom can we gain from Scripture about how we should view our identity and human relationships in light of Instagram, Twitter and Facebook?

The following pages are the best attempt I've found to provide a holistic exploration of the issues when it comes to social media. Neither wholly welcoming nor wholly dismissive, the book looks at the issues from new perspectives and gives relevant reflections on this modern-day phenomenon from within the biblical narrative. It's refreshing to read a Christian exploration of these issues that goes beyond the usual topics but also touches on wider issues, including consumerism, privacy, surveillance and anonymity.

CHINE MCDONALD
Director of Communications
Evangelical Alliance

INTRODUCTION

'If you want a definition of water, don't ask a fish.'

This old Chinese proverb has come to mind repeatedly as I've been writing this book. I've been using email and the web for twenty years, a mobile phone for fifteen, social media for ten. They've become an integral part of my work, my leisure time, my everyday existence. Like the rest of us, I'm thoroughly connected – and short of some kind of disaster we're only going to become even more connected in the coming years. The web and its associated technologies are a part of almost everything I do. How do you critique something that has become so inseparable from your life that you barely even consciously register it anymore?

When you come down to it, technologies are really only expressions of the properties of the world that God has created. When I started writing, it was therefore tempting to suggest that communications technologies in the round are as neutral as the laws of physics and maths on which they are built. Whilst this may arguably be true in its purest, most conceptual form, it soon became clear that this kind of simplification didn't do justice to the reality.

History of technology professor Melvin Kranzberg memorably put it: 'Technology is neither good nor bad; nor is it neutral.' The ethical impact of a technology is *always* subject to the ends of those who implement it. 'By that I mean that technology's interaction with the social ecology is such that technical developments frequently have environmental, social, and human consequences that go far beyond the immediate purposes of the technical devices and practices themselves, and the same technology can have quite different results when introduced into different contexts or under different circumstances.[1] The same can be said of the spiritual impact. A technology – like a social media platform – is implicitly the expression of the spiritual values of its creators and users, and will have spiritual outcomes, intended and unintended. Some are great; some unexpected; some terrible. The problem is discerning which is happening at any given time. This unprecedented connectivity can and often *does* help us to relate better – more openly, more justly, even more deeply, in a way that honours our mutual humanity and our status as God's creation. Humans are social animals. Relationship is core to what we are: we are created to communicate, and communications technology (it does what it says on the tin) allows us to achieve that better than ever before. Unfortunately, though, we're also fallen beings, prone to allowing it to have the opposite effect. It's part of what Francis Spufford, in his book *Unapologetic*, calls the HPtFtU, or Human Propensity to Mess things Up.[2]

Perhaps for that reason, something I've struggled with consistently throughout the book is appearing positive about the opportunities offered by these technologies. I am immensely positive – as will become abundantly clear; I use them daily and actively both for work and leisure and my life would look very different without them. But still, I find myself focusing on their downsides. We intuitively know how to use them in a beneficial way and do so all the time with very little encouragement required. The problem comes in our habits of also using them in harmful ways, which are overlaid on everything else like a patina of verdigris on

---

1 Melvin Kranzberg, 'Introduction: Technological and Cultural Change – Past, Present and Future' in *New Worlds, New Technologies, New Issues*, ed. Stephen H Sutcliffe, *Research in Technology Studies*, vol. 6 (Lehigh University Press, 1992), p. 100.

2 OK, but you get the general idea. See Francis Spufford, *Unapologetic: Why, despite everything, Christianity can still make surprising emotional sense* (Faber & Faber, 2013).

an old coin. Strip away what is not supposed to be there and you are left with something beautiful – something that was there all the time, but that was hidden under unwanted and unattractive accretions of corrosion, laid down due to years of neglect. Once we, in the words of one critic,[3] 'master its demonic assumptions' – overcome the ways that we unwittingly allow technology to undermine our faith and relationships – then we're left with what's good.

Doing the right thing is often a matter of not doing the wrong thing.

It's just that we're *really* good at doing the wrong thing.

This is why the Bible is still relevant to definitively contemporary questions about the impact of social networking and instant global mass communication: human nature remains stubbornly resistant to change, and although these technologies are unique to the twenty-first century, technological development itself is not – the ancient Israelites went through epoch-defining technological changes of their own. There really is nothing new under the sun with regards to our ability to foul up what should be our closest and most meaningful relationships, let alone all the others. Intentionally or unwittingly, engaging with these new communications technologies can and does erode and undermine our faith and our relationships with each other – the way we relate to each other being an integral part of our faith, according to Jesus.[4] Like all new technologies since the dawn of time, they can be used for benign or malign purposes. In this instance, the fact that they fly under the radar because they're woven through the fabric of our lives makes it so much harder to judge their impact. Often, like the Chinese fish, it doesn't even occur to us to question them. But when you think about it, how could something so all-pervasive and powerful – something that permeates literally every waking hour and every area of our lives – *not* have spiritual consequences?

---

3 Andrew Fellows, personal conversation.
4 Matthew 22:37–40.

It's a difficult, complicated matter to get to the bottom of, but at the heart of this book is a very simple question. The issue of who or what we trust and obey, the authority from which we consciously or unconsciously take our cues in all the decisions we make, is fundamental to every Christian's walk with God – but until we examine our habits, we may not even know the answer.

Who's in charge?

1. WHO'S IN CHARGE?

'WITH GREAT POWER COMES GREAT RESPONSIBILITY'[1]

I'd picked up on various articles in the national press about the curious phenomenon that is bitcoin – at once a currency, a piece of software, a decentralised movement and a paradigm for a radical redistribution of power – for a couple of years before I finally dipped my toes in the water at the beginning of 2014. The more I learnt, the more it became clear that this represented a once-in-a-generation technological shift that would have implications greater than any of us could see at the time, similar to the popularisation of personal computers or the rise of the internet.

Bitcoin was the first and is still the best-known and most-used of the literally hundreds of digital currencies that have sprung up since it was launched in 2009. But the implications of its development are far broader than for money alone. Cryptographic currencies, or cryptocurrencies, use blockchains – ledgers that record ownership and that are shared by everyone rather than held by a single, trusted party like a bank. Bitcoin and many other cryptocurrencies use a vast amount of processing power, pooled by all the computers in the network, to secure the ledger – meaning that no single computer or organisation would have the resources necessary to create a fraudulent transaction.

---

1 Uncle Ben, *Spider-Man* (Marvel Enterprises, 2002).

Computers are rewarded for delivering the calculations that validate each batch of transactions with new bitcoins.[2] It's a brilliant solution to the problem of transferring money online. The issue is that digital information can be copied easily, so without the blockchain, it would be impossible to know who owned what without a single ledger maintained by a central authority.

These networks therefore allow people to exchange information directly with each other, without any inter-mediaries. They operate outside of the existing financial system and without banks, governments, payment processors and any other third party to facilitate or control them. Anyone with an internet connection can send money – and potentially register property ownership, buy and sell shares in a company, record contracts, establish identity, crowdfund a project, and far more – without relying on anyone else.

Fascinated by the technology and the opportunities it offered, I learned as much as I could and quickly found there was a niche for someone who could communicate the complex ideas involved. It wasn't long before I was earning a significant proportion of my income in several different digital currencies by writing articles, white papers and film scripts, working as a communicator and consultant for businesses, communities and individuals scattered around the world.

Regulation always lags behind the technology it aims to police, and governments were only just starting to catch on to both the opportunities and risks posed by these new forms of money. Things have changed a lot now, but at the time it still had the reputation of being the Wild West.

---

2 This briefly describes the 'proof-of-work' approach used by bitcoin. See further in the bitcoin white paper, https://bitcoin.org/bitcoin.pdf. An increasing number of cryptocurrencies employ proof-of-stake and other related means of securing their blockchains.

It was like capitalism on steroids: an environment where anything went and there were few consequences in the real world. Unfettered by regulation and bureaucracy, innovation happened blindingly fast – but there were plenty of hacks and scams, too. On several occasions I witnessed millions of dollars' worth of digital cash being stolen due to poor security practices (even at the time of writing, one major exchange has just fallen victim to a $60 million hack), and new Ponzi schemes seemed to appear on a near-weekly basis.

I met and worked with some great people, many of whom were and are involved with the technology because they want to change the world and create a more just financial system. Many of those I knew were fiercely private, preserving their anonymity at all costs – some because they lived in hostile jurisdictions like Iran, China and Russia, some because they were paranoid, others because they wanted to avoid conflicts of interest with their day jobs, and others still because they were hiding criminal activity.

The blockchain is a hugely disruptive technology with far-reaching implications and the potential to shift the balance of power away from existing authorities and towards ordinary citizens, just as the web itself began to democratise access to information in the late 1990s and enabled people to circumvent the previous gatekeepers – such as news editors and media presenters – who controlled our access to information. My experiences were the perfect illustration of how technology is inherently about power. It enables you to do things that you couldn't do before, things that people who don't use it still can't do, things that maybe some people are keen you shouldn't do. That power can bring freedom – if nothing else, cryptocurrency is about freedom from the current structures of financial and administrative power. But it's an ideal that cuts both ways. The same technology that allows us to move funds cheaply and quickly around the globe for the first time in history, this technology that offers enormous benefits to the unbanked and to migrant workers, also opens up a whole new set of less benign opportunities.

What soon became clear to me was that the power and responsibility to carry out all kinds of activities that had previously been the preserve of governments and banks – to print money; to collect tax at source; to track, approve, block or reverse transactions; to audit accounts and demand information based on their content, to name a few – was now mine. If I'd wanted to, it would have been easy to hide a chunk of my earnings from the taxman.[3] To launder money and buy drugs without detection. To fund accounts on gambling sites anonymously. To purchase illegal weapons and pornography. Even to donate money to terrorist organisations or procure murder for hire. (The recent trial of Ross Ulbricht, the mastermind who ran the illegal online drugs marketplace the Silk Road, suggests that it's actually quite hard to find a reliable murderer for hire on the web.[4] Even so, the web is only 25 years old and already we're talking about paying for a hitman like it's ordering pizza. And googling almost any information you could ever need. And Gangnam Style.[5] We are *not* in Kansas any more.)

One of the critical things I learned is that you simply cannot give people that power – power offered not just by this specific set of technologies but by the web itself and communications technology more generally – without also giving them the ability to misuse it. The only way to prevent someone from abusing a particular power is for an authority to remove it from them, thereby disempowering them and

---

3 For the record, I never did.
4 http://arstechnica.com/tech-policy/2015/02/the-hitman-scam-dread-pirate-roberts-bizarre-murder-for-hire-attempts/
5 https://youtu.be/9bZkp7q19fo or google it.

giving that authority the opportunity to abuse it instead. We just can't have it both ways.

The question we have to ask, as individuals and collectively, is: Who do we want wielding the power?

The information revolution is unquestionably the most far-reaching advance of the twenty-first century: the development of fast, global, mass communication through the internet, smartphones and mobile devices. It is beyond any doubt that these technologies have already changed the way we work, communicate, shop, socialise, spend our leisure time and almost everything else. But disruptive new technologies have arisen periodically over the course of history and have always challenged existing social norms and the power structures surrounding them. The printing press, the radio, the automobile. Far enough in our past, the shift from nomadic hunter-gatherer groups to settled agricultural ones brought about fundamental changes.[6] In the ancient Near East in the second millennium BC, the development of the alphabet over more complex systems brought the possibility of widespread literacy.[7] For the early Israelites, there is also an obvious example in the material after which we have named that whole Age in history: Iron.

Most Christian approaches to the internet and communications technology focus on a small number of problem issues that arise

---

6   For an intriguing and detailed overview of why this happened the way it did on different continents, take a look at Jared Diamond's *Guns, Germs and Steel: A short history of everybody for the last 13,000 years* (Vintage, 1998).

7   Former Chief Rabbi Jonathan Sacks has argued that the simplified Hebrew alphabet posed an existential threat to bureaucratic and hierarchical societies like Egypt's. 'In ancient times – indeed in Europe until the invention of printing – the only class that was literate was the priesthood. "A kingdom of priests" thus meant, among other things, "a society of universal literacy".' See http://www.rabbisacks.org/covenant-conversation-5768-yitro-a-holy-nation/ and *The Dignity of Difference: How to Avoid the Clash of Civilizations* (Bloomsbury, 2003), pp. 125–41.

from the online world, as well as the opportunities for spreading the gospel. Whilst these are important, they are only the tip of the iceberg in terms of how these technologies affect our faith, and we need a broader approach to assess them. There is a far more profound and far-reaching issue at stake.

Technology is about power.
Technology is always about power.
And how that power is used has enormous consequences.

This is a book that aims to unpack some of those consequences, including the spiritual, with the hope of helping us use the vast array of communications technologies that saturate our existences in a way that aligns with our faith and, hopefully, makes us more faithful, more human, better at relating to one another. Many of the insights have been gathered by actively and enthusiastically – and sometimes deliberately – making mistakes, and wherever possible I've tried to give meaningful suggestions for application. No doubt you'll be able to think of plenty more, but I hope the ones included will provide a useful starting point.

Ultimately, then, this isn't a book about the internet or technology. It is about power and how it impacts our freedom as Christians. Freedom comes in different forms: physical, emotional/psychological, spiritual and financial. These often go together. The way we use and apply any technology has spiritual significance, in the same way that how we spend our money and use our time also has spiritual significance. The choices we make affect other people and they affect us, whether or not we recognise it. As well as the danger of allowing others to use technology to enslave us in one way or another, there is a risk that we allow ourselves to be involuntarily enslaved through our *own* use of it in a broad variety of ways we will be exploring. Engaging or choosing not to engage with technology is a moral and spiritual issue, because any technology applied in the real world necessarily embodies a set of values.

The comparison with ironworking in the Old Testament highlights this point well. The Philistines used their knowledge of ironworking to oppress the Israelites. They actively prevented the Israelites from acquiring the ability to smelt iron and create tools and weapons. Iron gave too great a military advantage for them to allow just anyone to use it.[8] In the hands of the Israelites, though, iron meant freedom.[9] Technology is power, information is power: power that we either take up for ourselves and others, or give away, with the risk that another party uses it against us.

OPPRESSIVE REGIMES

Egypt has a long history of the misuse of power, as the Bible shows. The Israelites spent many years in slavery under Pharaoh before the Exodus. What is interesting is that Egypt was originally the Israelites' salvation, the country that welcomed the starving family of Jacob and allowed them to settle and thrive. But over time, that situation changed, and the descendants of the refugees from Canaan became first resented and feared, and ultimately enslaved by their hosts.

---

8 'Sisera, the commander of [Jabin king of Canaan's] army ... had nine hundred chariots fitted with iron and had cruelly oppressed the Israelites for twenty years' (Judges 4:2–3). Judges 1:19 states that the Israelites were not successful in battle on the plains, implying that this is at least in part because their opponents had iron chariots. There are few mentions of the Israelites using swords in battle in the early history books; instead they use makeshift weapons and farming implements. This is probably because 'Not a blacksmith could be found in the whole land of Israel, because the Philistines had said, "Otherwise the Hebrews will make swords or spears!"' (1 Samuel 13:19).

9 See 1 Samuel 13:19–22. There are differing theories as to why iron replaced bronze (e.g. because it was more abundant, better suited to weaponry, or due to disruption of the supply of tin that was required for bronze). Either way, these verses show that the Philistines deliberately restricted ironworking in Israel to maintain their control over the population.

By the time of Moses, Egypt had become a brutal dictatorship in which Pharaoh held ultimate power. The king was considered a deity, the intermediary between the pantheon of Egyptian gods and the ordinary people. He was also supreme military commander and the head of government. There was a cadre of elite priests who enjoyed privileged positions, and they were the only ones aside from Pharaoh who owned any land (Genesis 47:22). As well as running the temples and conducting sacrifices, the priests were the nation's bureaucrats, since unlike the majority of the population they had the time and training to master the complex writing system of hieroglyphics.

Power was centralised around these leaders by controlling information (few people could read or write), maintaining a large standing army, through bureaucracy, land management, tax collection and labour, and through religious beliefs and practice. Land was said to belong ultimately to the gods, for example, who needed placating with regular sacrifices through the extensive temple system. The vast majority of the population were farmers who worked land owned by the state or the priests. Artisans had higher social status, but still essentially worked for the state.

In this way, every form of power was concentrated around Pharaoh and the group of priests and scribes who ruled the kingdom: religious, financial, military and judicial power. The injustices allowed by this system culminated in the deaths of Israelite baby boys when the growing Israelite population seemed to Pharaoh and the Egyptians to represent a threat to their existing way of life (Exodus 1). Centralised power didn't mean this was inevitable, of course – it just meant that there was no way to stop that abuse of power. Centralised power is unaccountable. The extent of the people's submission to Pharaoh is evident from the effectiveness of his decree: 'Then Pharaoh gave this order to all his people: "Every boy that is born [to the Hebrews] you must throw into the Nile, but let every girl live!"' (Exodus 1:22)

NOT LIKE EGYPT: PHYSICAL AND RELIGIOUS FREEDOM

The Israelites experienced a certain kind of government and structure of society many times over throughout their history, though particularly so during their formative years in Egypt. So perhaps it is not surprising that the rules given to them by God by which they would govern their own political and economic systems were very different. These rules have enduring significance because they embodied principles such as justice and faithfulness that we see throughout the Bible – and they have continuing application for our approach to communications technologies today.

The Exodus account acknowledges that the misuse of power the Israelites experienced in Egypt was more than just physical slavery. Harsh manual labour was one aspect of it, but they were denied other freedoms too. They did not have financial independence, as had been the case for most of Egypt for centuries.[10] They certainly did not have the freedom to worship God – Pharaoh explicitly refused them the right to make sacrifices in the desert (Exodus 5), and his tactic of working them harder was meant to dampen their enthusiasm for worship (Exodus 5:6–9). Fill their days with work, seems to be his logic, and you remove the opportunity to think about such things. This has clear resonance with the way our Always-On culture squeezes out the time and inclination for faith.

Although it is nowhere explicitly stated in the Bible that the Old Testament Law and organisation of society constituted a deliberate policy to be comprehensively Not Like Egypt, this was essentially their effect. In many different regards, Israel was the anti-Egypt: a place of political, financial and religious freedom, rather than slavery. Given Pharaoh's near-absolute control over the population, it's not hard to see why this was important for

---

10 See Genesis 47:20–26.

the Israelites. Religious freedom goes hand-in-hand with other freedoms.[11]

Moreover, from the other side of the coin, taking away another person's freedoms without just reason is incompatible with a meaningful faith, since faith is a matter of right relationship with God and with other people. When Jesus is asked what the most important law is, he answers not in terms of sacrifice or giving or prayer, but in the language and framework of relationships: '"Love the Lord your God with all your heart and with all your soul and with all your mind." This is the first and greatest commandment. And the second is like it: "Love your neighbour as yourself." All the Law and the Prophets hang on these two commandments.' (Matthew 22:37–40) In other words, every law in the Bible, from obscure regulations about beards and shellfish to rules concerning adultery and murder, is designed to address some aspect of some relationship. The whole narrative of the Bible is about God's relationship with us – created, fractured, patched up, repeatedly tested to breaking point and finally restored, across the span of thousands of years.

This emphasis on right relationships is one of the key reasons there were to be no unnecessary concentrations of power in Israel. For example, legal cases were heard by local courts, with only the hardest cases being passed up to higher authorities (see Deuteronomy 17:8–13 and Exodus 18:18–26). In Egypt, there was no separate judicial system. The 'judges' were government officials – and they did not appear to have a developed legal code to which to turn for guidance. Pharaoh was the head of the legal system – there was no 'separation of powers' here. Instead of a god-king like Egypt's Pharaoh, Israel was not supposed to have a king at all (1 Samuel 8). The laws laid out about the king, which God would

---

11   This is emphatically not to say that those caught in one or other form of slavery cannot have a real and vibrant faith, as was the case with many African slaves in America. However, the loss of personal autonomy inevitably reduces the ability to express your faith fully.

eventually give to the Israelites as a concession, stated that he was to be subject to the Law, not above it. He was also limited in the wealth, possessions and military capability he was personally able to accumulate:

> *The king, moreover, must not acquire great numbers of horses for himself or make the people return to Egypt to get more of them, for the LORD has told you, 'You are not to go back that way again.' He must not take many wives, or his heart will be led astray. He must not accumulate large amounts of silver and gold.*
>
> *When he takes the throne of his kingdom, he is to write for himself on a scroll a copy of this law, taken from that of the Levitical priests. It is to be with him, and he is to read it all the days of his life so that he may learn to revere the LORD his God and follow carefully all the words of this law and these decrees and not consider himself better than his fellow Israelites and turn from the law to the right or to the left. Then he and his descendants will reign a long time over his kingdom in Israel.*

DEUTERONOMY 17:16–20

The priests had responsibilities and power that could be abused, of course (1 Samuel 2:12–17), but there *was* a separation of powers between priesthood and kingship, and the Levites were dispersed all over the country to serve in different capacities – in public health, law and finance as well as religious matters, playing the role of something like public servants. They were also reliant on donations and funded by the Temple, rather than possessing an allocation of land – alone among the Israelites and in stark contrast to the wealthy and land-owning Egyptian priests. This helped to prevent a centralisation of land and wealth around the priesthood.

The only events that typically required a response on the national level were wars and threats of invasion. Between the state and the individual were a series of intermediary groups who were entrusted with different responsibilities. These groups included the extended family, the community (village or town) and the tribe. The principle of Subsidiarity in Catholic Social Teaching[12] reflects this idea of decentralised power – or rather, of appropriate decentralisation. No decision or action is taken by a higher, more centralised authority if a lower, more local one can deal with it better. The more centralised an authority, the more distant it is from its citizens, the less it understands their needs and the more likely it is to neglect or even harm them. Needlessly centralised authority takes initiative and control away from its people, doing for them tasks that they can better carry out themselves because they understand their circumstances better – and they have a direct interest in the outcome.

As well as limiting the concentration of political power, Israel's laws limited the concentration of financial power. In Egypt, a wealthy elite owned all the land and farmers paid them to be allowed to work it and grow crops. In Israel, everyone had access to a plot of land that belonged to their family forever. Even if they were forced to sell it due to temporary hardship, it was to be returned to them every fiftieth year, in the Jubilee (Leviticus 25 – though it is unclear to what degree this was carried out in practice).

Not only that, but the laws around money lending were designed to prevent cases of long-term poverty, which would lead to loss of land. No one was allowed to charge interest to a fellow Israelite. The reason for this was because taking a loan was supposed to be a last-ditch solution to poverty. Charging interest was seen as a way of extracting money from people who were already poor, enriching the wealthy at the expense of the vulnerable. (Poverty

---

12 Catholic Social Teaching is an extensive and detailed body of thought on issues of social justice, developed from biblical principles and the teachings of early Christian thinkers.

was, additionally, one of the principle routes into slavery – as happened to the people of Egypt in Genesis 47:15–24.) Interest was seen as a form of injustice, locking the borrower further into his poverty rather than relieving it and giving him and his family a chance of economic independence again. This is reflected by the idea in Proverbs,

> Whoever increases wealth by taking interest or profit from the poor amasses it for another, who will be kind to the poor.
>
> PROVERBS 28:8

Whereas we see credit as a form of freedom – a way of bringing forward future earnings to today – the Bible sees it as a form of oppression. 'The rich rule over the poor, and the borrower is slave to the lender' (Proverbs 22:7). It's an incidental point, but we buy so much on credit nowadays that acquiring consumer electronic goods or anything else can have this side effect of putting us in a kind of modern-day debt slavery.

The Exodus was God's act of liberation for the Israelites from their slavery in Egypt. Everything about the nation they were to create was to be different from the harshness and injustice that they had experienced under Pharaoh. Their ideals for their politics and their economy were the opposite of those in Egypt's centralised and abusive dictatorship, even if those ideals were not always worked out in practice. Even the form of 'slavery' they practised was more like bonded servitude, part of the welfare system, rather than the brutal and dehumanising ownership that occurred in Egypt.

The reason for the Bible's limits on the concentration of human power can be summed up in the words of the nineteenth century politician and historian, Lord Acton: 'Power tends to corrupt, and absolute power corrupts absolutely. Great men are almost always bad men.' God, not Pharaoh or any other human agency, was supposed to be Israel's final authority. Ultimate power belonged to him alone. This is why the Israelites working on the Sabbath and asking for a king of their own were seen in such a dim light: they represented a voluntary return to the conditions of slavery from which God had rescued them, trivialising his work of redemption and displaying ingratitude at his grace.

The biblical scepticism around the concentration of power is keenly relevant to aspects of the information revolution, including issues of privacy and surveillance. This access to new capabilities is also why we must be careful with the way we use communications technologies and allow them into our lives. They offer amazing benefits and freedoms, but that power is a double-edged blade. They give us unprecedented control over many aspects of our lives, but at the same time there is the very real risk that we give up control at the same time. The three areas explored in the next three chapters of this book – headspace, time and integrity – suggest that it is very easy to give away elements of our autonomy when we uncritically adopt communications technologies, and thereby implicitly allow them to undermine our faith.

THE CHALLENGE FOR US: WHO IS IN CHARGE?

In Egypt the Israelites were kept in slavery, losing their physical, financial and spiritual freedoms under Pharaoh. And yet, for all the hardships of slavery, the Bible notes that there were compensations – ones that the Israelites remembered all too quickly after the Exodus.

> *The whole Israelite community set out from Elim and came to the Desert of Sin, which is between Elim and Sinai, on the fifteenth day of the second month after they had come out of Egypt. In the desert the whole community grumbled against Moses and Aaron. The*

> Israelites said to them, 'If only we had died by the LORD's
> hand in Egypt! There we sat around pots of meat and
> ate all the food we wanted, but you have brought us out
> into this desert to starve this entire assembly to death.'
>
> EXODUS 16:1–3

God gives them manna, but they later complain that this is not
enough:

> The rabble with them began to crave other food, and
> again the Israelites started wailing and said, 'If only we
> had meat to eat! We remember the fish we ate in Egypt
> at no cost – also the cucumbers, melons, leeks, onions
> and garlic. But now we have lost our appetite; we never
> see anything but this manna!'
>
> NUMBERS 11:4–6

We might have a picture of the Israelites as underfed slaves in
Egypt, but their vivid memories of their diet in captivity suggest
otherwise. Presumably, the Egyptians were investing in their
workforce, knowing that starving prisoners are both dangerous
and unproductive. Just six weeks into their newly-found freedom
from a lifetime of harsh slavery and the systematic extermination
of their sons, the Israelites realised that being on their own meant
taking responsibility for their own wellbeing and futures, and
concluded: Life wasn't so bad in Egypt.

Why is submitting unquestioningly to the loss of autonomy
wrong? There are probably a few reasons, but somewhere at the top
of the list is that being a slave necessarily reduces your freedoms,
meaning that you may not always be able to act according to your
conscience. The Israelites were denied the freedom to worship
God in the way they wanted, and the opportunity to rest on the
Sabbath. Their complaints and longing for the lives they had left
behind in Egypt were indicative of their attitude to the God who
had redeemed them.

We have been freed from the slavery of sin by Christ's sacrifice (Romans 6:17–18). We have also been freed in an earthly way from the tyranny of constant work. Communications technologies are time-saving and labour-saving. Used wisely, they can bring a high degree of freedom. Used indiscriminately and unquestioningly, they create and facilitate a never-ending stream of work, paid and unpaid, that distracts us and drains our time. This, of course, is just another form of slavery. It shows that we are not really in charge of the technology we use. And that suggests that we are, tacitly or explicitly, willing to allow it to take a piece of the allegiance we otherwise reserve for God. In biblical terms, we allow our smartphones and online habits to become idols.

This presents a challenge to every Christian, whether as an individual or organisation. We may have made mistakes that set us on a particular trajectory. Will we continue to follow it? In Genesis, Cain brought an offering that God found unfavourable.

> *So Cain was very angry, and his face was downcast.*
> *Then the LORD said to Cain, 'Why are you angry? Why*
> *is your face downcast? If you do what is right, will you*
> *not be accepted? But if you do not do what is right, sin*
> *is crouching at your door; it desires to have you, but you*
> *must rule over it.*

GENESIS 4:5–7

God gave Cain the opportunity to change, to master the sin that threatened to consume him. When confronted, though, he deliberately chose a different course.

The ability to communicate online is so much a part of the world around us that we often do not question the place it has in our lives. We simply absorb these facilities into our lives without asking what their true impacts might be. If we *do* recognise their effects, we are often reactive in our response, rather than deliberately setting out to use them for a particular reason.

The challenge, then, is to be deliberate in our use of communications technologies, knowing that either we will master them or they will master us. The impact of technology is not merely technological: it is relational and spiritual. The way we engage with it reflects the answer to the question that is so key for our faith: who is really in charge?

Throughout this book, many of the suggestions for application are aimed at the individual level – things we can each do as part of our personal engagement with the issues raised by communications technology and the way we exercise the power it gives us. However, we live in community and our decisions and actions affect other people. If you have the opportunity, discuss the points raised here and throughout this book as part of a community of faith, recognising that a joint exploration will enable a fuller engagement with the issues and greater accountability for any decisions you make.

1. *Start with an online audit.* Take a sheet of paper and divide it into 168 boxes, 24 for each day of the week. Fill in each box with your typical activity for that hour – sleep, work, meals, exercise, recreation, and so on. Now, mark the times you use digital media in various different ways, whether that is searching/surfing the web, email, instant messaging, social media, TV/video, and so on. (This may be easier to do as you go along, rather than in retrospect.) You may find that one slot is occupied by more than one category – e.g. you may use social media on your smartphone at the same time as watching TV.

Total your results. Is the time you spend in different activities online more or less than you expected? Does this result prompt a response?

2. *Tally the number of times you are interrupted* or distracted from another conversation or activity over the course of a day by your smartphone, social media and other messaging. What is the effect of this?

3. *Ask that fundamental question: Who is in charge?* Who holds the power in this instance? Does technology genuinely serve ends in line with your faith, or are there times when it undermines your relationship with God and other people? If so, there may be clear areas to address.

4. *Consider the effect* of how using the web, computers and mobile devices is changing and shaping your behaviour, across many different aspects of life – both good and bad. Compare how you act now with how you might act without access to it. In what ways do they give you greater freedom? In what ways do they reduce your freedom?

5. *What positive qualities* does communications technology bring to your life, both in the conveniences it allows and in the changes you see in the way you relate to people? Conversely, how does it damage your life and relationships? Think of the ways you can redeem these technologies by deliberately using them to further your faith and relationships, rather than using them uncritically.

6. For organisations, including churches:

   • *What does it mean for technology to serve you?* Christians have often been slow to adopt new technologies, and churches can be behind the times (frequently down to a lack of funding) – although there are, equally, churches that have leveraged communications technology to great effect. Are there ways in which technology could be used to carry out a more effective ministry – opportunities you are missing to engage with people? That might include anything from having a website that is fit for purpose and enabling people to donate money and set up standing orders online to recording or videoing talks for download, keeping people informed via social media as well as email lists, and so on.

- *Are there areas in which technology works against your goals?* Do you need to adopt new ways of working? It could be that emails have unnecessarily replaced face-to-face communication in the office or with your congregation, perhaps because of the convenience this offers but at the expense of deeper and more meaningful communication. It could be that use of technology alienates some people, because they are not as tech-savvy. Is technology used to strengthen relationships, or does it tend to make them 'thinner', less real and meaningful?

What's the first thing you do when you wake up in the morning? Grab a shower? Put the coffee on? Say a prayer? Read the Bible?

Or perhaps, like 80 per cent of smartphone owners, one of your very first actions is to reach for your mobile and check for email and updates. Odds on it will also be the last thing you do at night, too, and an average of every 5 to 10 minutes in between.

We live in an Always-On culture: we spend our lives online, connected to the web and to each other through our phones, tablets, laptops and desktop computers, and plenty of other devices besides. Most of us are so immersed in our online world that we barely question the impact it has on our faith – or even whether it has an effect at all (back to the Chinese fish's myopic definition of water).

The amount of time we spend online and how unquestioningly we do so doesn't necessarily make it wrong, but it does highlight something of the power this technology can hold over us – and of our implicit priorities.

2. ALWAYS-ON

HOW BEING CONNECTED ALL THE TIME ISN'T GOOD FOR OUR CONNECTEDNESS

L'Abri, French for 'The Shelter', is a Christian community founded by Francis Schaeffer to offer students and other travellers a safe place to explore religious and philosophical ideas. It includes a strong emphasis on living together, with students participating in communal meals and contributing to the running of the organisation (e.g. by helping with cooking and maintenance) as well as spending time in private study and taking part in discussion groups.

We're not a retreat or a monastic community, but we do try to maintain a degree of separation from the world. We didn't want to make it impossible to communicate with family and the outside world, but we did want to make sure it remains a haven for the people who come here. For many years we had no TV, only a newspaper, and a payphone people would queue to use. We'd show one film a week and discuss it afterwards. That was pretty much the same from the 1970s up to the mid-1990s.

The biggest changes we've seen over time are in people's eating habits – their awareness of their diet – and of course their relationship with media technology. It became noticeable around fifteen years ago. Because many of our students came from abroad it was hard for them to access email and the web in those days – it was before 3G networks and low-cost international data, and we didn't have a shared

Wi-Fi connection for their laptops. They would undergo a kind of detox from email and text messages, sometimes becoming quite anxious for a while. In work time, we found that people often listened to their iPods, which cut them off from others; the aim is that people discuss the ideas they've learned in the context of the day-to-day life of the community.

Those changes have accelerated in recent years, with smartphones and 3G and 4G connections. We have seen this profoundly affect students' ability to concentrate and participate in the community. Their attention spans are much shorter. More than just a compulsion to use social networking or email, the impression is that people have an addiction to these devices themselves. Most of the men are either dabbling in or addicted to internet pornography. We don't ask them to give up their smartphones, because these devices have become almost an extension of ourselves now, and it would be invasive to do so. But we are increasingly struggling against these changes, because students' capacity for reflection is impaired. It breaks down the quality of relationships.

We now have a seminar early on in students' time here, to discuss the idea of community and the effects that communications technology has on our regular relationships. And we notice the biggest changes in people who have been here for several months. After a term or so, students seem to come alive, intellectually. They're more critically discerning of media. It's as if they wake up. However they engage with social media and the web in the future – and many will change their approach based on their time here – that abstention is necessary in order to be able to think critically about it.'

Andrew Fellows, former director of *L'Abri*, UK

You know the way it goes: there's an electronic chirp, or a discreet buzz, and you're reflexively reaching into your pocket for your phone. It doesn't matter where you are or what you're doing – at work, in conversation, eating a meal, watching TV, hanging out with friends, perhaps even at church or praying – your hand has probably moved before you've had time to think. If you don't recognise that behaviour in yourself (congratulations!), you'll almost certainly have been on the other side of it.

The communications technologies that now permeate our every waking moment are sold to us on the premise they make our lives better, and individually and initially they often do. Imagine having to phone that friend and congratulate them on their new job rather than texting them or posting an update on their timeline. Imagine having to send a letter instead of firing off an email, then waiting for the reply – a week-long round trip instead of minutes or hours. But, of course, it's not that simple. I have a lot more 'friends' on social media than I do actual real-life friends – the kind of people I might actually meet up with for coffee or hang out with, let alone the ones I could rely on to bail me out of the police station at 2 am or drive me across the country to a family funeral. And an email is not simply an electronic letter. I send far more emails in the average day than I ever sent letters in a month. 'e-Letter' is just a tiny intersection in what is represented by the sprawling, hungry Venn diagram circle marked 'email'.

FROM ZX TO LOL

> You see – wire telegraph is a kind of a very, very long cat. You pull his tail in New York and his head is meowing in Los Angeles. Do you understand this? And radio operates exactly the same way: You send signals here, and they receive them there. The only difference is that there is no cat.

ATTRIBUTED, QUITE POSSIBLY ERRONEOUSLY, TO ALBERT EINSTEIN.

For what it's worth in terms of writing credentials for this subject, I happen to occupy an ambiguous vantage point in the history of the information revolution. Like other people my age, I grew up in a world that was, by today's standards, profoundly un-connected. My earliest experience with computers included waiting for rudimentary platform games like *Donkey Kong* or impenetrable text adventures like *The Hobbit* to load via audio tape drive on one of Clive Sinclair's iconic ZX Spectrum 48k computers.[13] It took five minutes of watching stripes scroll up and down the sides of the screen and listening to a weird range of electronic pulses, and if the volume on the tape player was wrong you had to start again.

Thinking about it, waiting around was involved in a lot of things we did. There were four TV channels and you watched programmes when they were on, or else you missed them forever. National phone calls were more expensive than local ones, unless you waited until the evening. Meeting up with people meant agreeing a time and place in advance and sticking to the plan, or you simply got left behind. If you wanted pictures of humorously-posed cats you had to convince the cat to participate, take a photo yourself and wait a week for the chemist to develop a blurry sepia version of it.

But the times, they were most definitely a-changing. By the time I was in my mid-teens the internet was taking hold, though you still had to connect to it via a dial-up connection that sounded comfortably reminiscent of the ZX Spectrum. When I went to university in 1997 email was already the default means of communicating at a distance but barely anyone had mobile phones. A few years later I was the proud owner of one of the world's 126 million Nokia 3310 'bricks'. Then the pace of change really accelerated and in just a handful more years it was all there: YouTube, eBay and Amazon, legal and illegal file sharing, smartphones, social networking. Unlimited information, instant communication, at your fingertips twenty-four hours a day. Wow.

---

13   ProTip: get Thorin to do most of the heavy lifting.

We found new reasons to use our computers and smartphones, and new forms of content to consume. Although traditional computers were better suited to creating material, tablets and smartphones – compact, portable and with touch screens instead of mice and keyboards – were well-suited to consuming it. And that is exactly what we did. Voraciously. Social networking connected us with hundreds or thousands of other people, whilst photo and video-sharing services not only served us images and movies but suggested the next ones we might want to view, producing a never-ending feed of information: what other people were doing, news, education, trivia, entertainment and much, much more.

I'm not the first person to look back and wonder what happened. Not in a particularly nostalgic sense, because smartphones and e-commerce and Skype and social networking and digital cash are really, really cool and I have a sneaking suspicion that the 80s weren't quite what they were cracked up to be. But I feel a justifiable sense of unease as well as an immense appreciation for the technology that, after all, I both thoroughly enjoy using and rely on to make a living.

My kids have never known the world without the web. Almost every aspect of their lives will be digitised and stored online. Like the rest of us, they will be connected 24/7, except they're far less likely to question whether it's a good thing or not, or even whether there's another way to *be*. They're going to be so much a part of the Matrix that they won't even know they're plugged in. It's going to have huge implications for the way they live their lives and relate to me and to each other – not least that they'll soon be asking for smartphones, and I'm going to be hard-pressed to take the moral high ground in telling them not to use them at the table.

HEADSPACE

So we're suddenly really connected and really well-informed. So what? Is that really a bad thing? If faith is ultimately about relationship then doesn't being more connected mean we're also better at relating?

As ever, these things are not a binary matter of right or wrong. The never-ending stream of information has both positive and negative implications. The 'Always-On' nature of life means that we can check in with a friend easily, or gather the information required to make a wise purchase, or save a couple of hours at work and get home in time to read the kids a bedtime story. Or it means we can be deluged with content we somehow feel duty-bound to consume, distracting us from real life and real interactions in favour of incessant updates.

Marshall McLuhan coined the term 'The medium is the message', by which he meant that delivery mechanism and format strongly influences how content is perceived. McLuhan went so far as to suggest that 'the "content" of a medium is like the juicy piece of meat carried by the burglar to distract the watchdog of the mind.'[14] Social media often encourages us to engage with the platform, not primarily its content. There will always be new messages; it is the medium *itself* that can be addictive.

In the broadest spiritual terms, the headspace this either grants or denies us resonates with Jesus' teaching in the Sermon on the Mount. 'No one can serve two masters. Either you will hate the one and love the other, or you will be devoted to the one and despise the other. You cannot serve both God and the constant feed of information' (Matthew 6:24, my paraphrase; the example Jesus uses is money, but an idol is an idol whether it comes in the form of a statue, a bank balance or a shiny touchscreen). Paul says something much the same in 1 Corinthians 6:12–13 – this time in the context of sex, but again, mastery is mastery, regardless of who or what is doing the mastering.

The 'two masters' idea isn't just an expression or an allegory. The bad master does have a tangible reality to it – not necessarily

---

14   Marshall McLuhan, *Understanding Media: The Extensions of Man* (MIT Press, 1964), p. 18.

in the guise of a pointy-tailed pitchfork-wielding entity, though I maintain there is a spiritual dimension to our use of technology – but in the sense that the playing field is deliberately slanted against us. There is a principle known as Parkinson's Law (after Cyril Northcote Parkinson, who coined it after his experience in the Civil Service), that 'work expands so as to fill the time available for its completion'. A variation of this principle could be stated for the content that we consume on our computers, tablets and smartphones. There is literally no end to it, and the danger is that the time we devote to it expands to meet the supply. And, like so many other things, business interests drive that behaviour.

> *US adults still spend considerably more time with TV than with any other single medium, and in 2014, they'll be in front their televisions for an average of 4 hours 28 minutes per day ... Combining online and mobile devices, however, eMarketer expects US adults to spend 5 hours 46 minutes with digital media daily this year, increasing digital's lead over television to well over 1 hour per day. Digital media, in our definition, includes all online, mobile and other nonmobile connected-device activities, such as video streamed through over-the-top services.*[15]

The more time we spend on a site, the more profitable it is for the company behind it. Powerful techniques have been developed to make sites more 'sticky', one of which is constantly serving new content – as well as organising existing content and presenting it in such a way as to encourage us to explore it. News outlets and sites like Wikipedia are particularly good at this, as is YouTube, which will make recommendations tailored to our tastes, based on our profile and previous viewing.

---

15 http://www.emarketer.com/Article/Mobile-Continues-Steal-Share-of-US-Adults-Daily-Time-Spent-with-Media/1010782

The effects of this tendency are not only anecdotally true, as in the story about newcomers arriving at *L'Abri* at the beginning of this chapter, but something that can be observed and measured. People's surfing habits are now well-known to change their neural pathways.

The repercussions of these changes have been tested and tested again by researchers, so we have a pretty good basis to say that the smallest of environmental stimuli are capable of stealing away our attention. With multiple browser tabs, mobile devices, and a constant connection to friends and information from the Internet, they're likely to jump from one activity to another in an instant. You might call this multi-tasking, but scientists call it a problem.

A 2009 Stanford study concluded that people who were incessantly plugged into the internet were 'suckers for irrelevancy'. Media multi-taskers performed poorly compared to the test subjects that weren't frequently online in three different tests that gauged their memory and monitored how they filtered out irrelevant stimuli and switched between tasks. 'The high multi-taskers are always drawing from all the information in front of them. They can't keep things separate in their minds.'[16]

The minds of chronic media multi-taskers do not function as well as they could.

When they're in situations where there are multiple sources of information coming from the external world or emerging out of memory, they're not able to filter out

---

16 See Digital Trends, 'The Internet Is Rewiring Your Brain And You Don't Even Know It', http://www.digitaltrends.com/social-media/the-internet-is-rewiring-our-brains-we-just-dont-realize-it/. See also http://www.huffingtonpost.com/2013/10/30shocking-ways-internet-rewires-brain_n_4136942.html

what's not relevant to their current goal ... That failure to filter means they're slowed down by that irrelevant information.[17]

Not only that, but many of us start to feel jittery if we lose access to that constant stream of updates. 'If you're being deluged by constant communication, the pressure to answer immediately is quite high,' and there can be a 'terrific anxiety about being out of the loop'.[18]

As an aside, it turns out that anxiety is the next item after the 'two masters' passage in the Sermon on the Mount.

Therefore I tell you, do not worry about your life, what you will eat or drink; or about your body, what you will wear. Is not life more than food, and the body more than clothes? Look at the birds of the air; they do not sow or reap or store away in barns, and yet your heavenly Father feeds them. Are you not much more valuable than they? Can any one of you by worrying add a single hour to your life?

MATTHEW 6:25–27

It's worth asking ourselves what our anxiety-driven instant-response actually achieves. There are few occasions when a delay of a few minutes before viewing an update makes any difference at all – and all too often there's a subtle cost. Taking out a phone becomes a kind of behavioural tic, even a psychological dependence.

This 'addiction' to technology prompted one enterprising group of people to create a successful Kickstarter crowdfunding campaign for the NoPhone: an iPhone-shaped piece of black plastic that is sold as a surrogate phone.

---

17 http://news.stanford.edu/news/2009/august24/multitask-research-study-082409.html
18 'The Internet Is Rewiring Your Brain And You Don't Even Know It.'

The idea of the NoPhone spawned from a night at a bar where we regularly hang out and socialize. And by "socialize", we mean stare at our phones and occasionally look up from our screens to order another round, which is the norm nowadays.

We see it everywhere. Couples on dates illuminated not by candles, but by glowing screens. Concerts where you can only see the performer through the attempted videography of the people standing in front of you. We're so addicted, just the feeling of a phone in our hands is comforting. So we decided to create the NoPhone; a satirical security blanket of sorts, meant to comment on our present addiction to technology. However, after we created the project, the response from people actually wanting to purchase the NoPhone was overwhelming.

We are selling the NoPhone to give the people what they want, a life of direct eye contact and improved conversational skills. A life beyond a smartphone. A life of NoPhone.[19]

Something that started as a joke and developed into a small business reflects the dawning realisation that many of us have – that technology supposed to help us connect with each other and improve our productivity is really distancing us from each other, undermining our relationships and sapping our free time. The philosopher Martin Buber wrote that the 'I-Thou'[20] relationship is paramount, that relationships with other people bring us into relationship with God. Compromising our ability to relate by sensitising the mind to distraction undermines our ability to love – and that includes love for God.

---

19   http://award.designtoimprovelife.dk/nomination/91
20   Martin Buber, *Ich und Du*, 1927 (translated as *I and Thou*, 1937).

'THIN' RELATIONSHIPS

Social media and communications technology can be a great way to maintain relationships, keeping in touch with people we wouldn't otherwise see very often. And online communities can offer real help for people who don't have those supportive networks of relationships in real life (see Chapter 4, Who Are You?). But too often these prevent us from relating to each other in a genuine way. The stream of content distracts us from spending time with each other, face to face. Even when we are engaging with other people online, rather than viewing other content, the nature of the relationship involved may be very different to that in real life.

Relationships are typically 'thinner' online, meaning that we do not have the breadth of interaction we usually have in person. They may be carried out in text only, and much of the context we take for granted in an offline relationship will be missing. There are also far more of them, and basic maths tells you that you can't sustain a large number of relationships as well as you can sustain a smaller number; despite our 24/7 online culture, there are still only twenty-four hours in a day. Critically, physical presence and touch are absent. There is a growing body of evidence that indicates how important these are for physical and psychological health. Attachment is a fundamental human need, particularly at the beginning of life but also throughout it. Touch is an integral part of our earliest relationships and many later ones; our closest relationships tend to feature touch to a greater or lesser extent. Touch is arguably the most emotionally significant of the senses.

The term 'thinner' relationships doesn't just refer to the lack of the rich array of cues we have to understand a person properly in face-to-face relationships – posture, body language, tone of voice, facial expression as well as the actual *content* of their words – though most of us have had the experience of misunderstanding something in a text message or email that was meant to be taken as a joke. Dunbar's Number is a suggested limit to the number of stable relationships the human brain is capable of maintaining, where not only each person is known but also *how they relate to one another* – as has been the case in communities since the dawn of time. A value of around 150 is generally proposed, and has found resonance in anything from the average number of people living in a Neolithic farming village to the optimal size of a modern company.

But our online 'communities' are not communities in this sense. Whereas once upon a time we might only have known a few dozen people really well and spent significant time with them, online we may have many hundreds or even thousands of friends, followers or connections. It is simply impossible to maintain all of these 'relationships' properly. One of the reasons for that is, as implied by Dunbar's theory, truly knowing someone is not just about knowing *them* – it's about understanding how they relate to other people, or what has been called Multiplexity.[21] I gain an extra insight into you by seeing how you interact with my friend, with your wife, with a boss or colleague. As C S Lewis poignantly remarked, the death of a mutual friend diminished his relationship with J R R Tolkien. 'Now that Charles is dead, I shall never again see Ronald's [Tolkien's] reaction to a specifically Charles joke. Far from having more of Ronald, having him "to myself" now that Charles is away, I have less of Ronald ...'.[22]

So-called networks of relationships online are not really networks: they are more hub-and-spokes affairs. I connect with everyone, and I might have some sense of who else each of my connections is connected to, but I don't have much of a sense of *how well* those people know each other – and my relationships with them are poorer as a result. We exchange a small number of deep relationships for a large number of superficial ones. Maintaining

21 See chapter 3, 'Relational Proximity', in Michael Schluter and David Lee, *The R Factor* (Hodder & Stoughton, 1993).
22 C S Lewis, *The Four Loves* (HarperCollins, 2002), chapter 4, Friend-ship.

relationships, online and offline, becomes an exercise a bit like spinning plates – spending just enough time with someone to show you're not willing to let them drop, rather than progressing the friendship meaningfully.

SERVING THE RIGHT MASTER

So far this chapter may have seemed a little pessimistic, which isn't the intention. There's lots of good that comes out of our Always-On culture, but we have to recognise technology is power, and as well as the many ways we can use it to affirm and strengthen our faith and relationships, it also has a tendency to get in the way of them. As Melvin Kranzberg said, 'Technology is neither good nor bad; nor is it neutral':[23] the impact is dependent on the *way* that the technology is implemented, the vision inherent in that expression, and how it's used in practice. As a result, how or whether we engage with Twitter might be different to our approach to Facebook, Instagram or LinkedIn. They are all social networks, but they encourage different patterns of engagement and relationship from their users.

Twitter, for example, with its 140-character message limit, is not suited for in-depth discussions. Used on its own, it tends to reduce debate to sound-bites. However, due to the nature of the platform it can be a good way to make contact with people or to keep track of developments; Twitter has become a source of breaking news from citizen journalists. Many situations have been covered from the ground in a way that mainstream media outlets cannot or do not. These include unfolding terrorist attacks such as the Boston Marathon bombings, and news of protests such as the 2014 Hong

---

23 Melvin Kranzberg, 'Introduction: Technological and Cultural Change – Past, Present and Future' in *New Worlds, New Technologies, New Issues*, ed. Stephen H Sutcliffe. *Research in Technology Studies*, vol. 6 (Lehigh University Press, 1992), p. 100, as discussed in the Introduction to this book (in case you skipped it).

Kong Umbrella Revolution, that would otherwise have been suppressed by local government-controlled media.

Other platforms place greater emphasis on photos and videos, such as Instagram, which was acquired by Facebook in 2012. Anecdotal evidence and empirical studies have shown that people feel pressure to present their best side in photos and updates uploaded to Facebook, presenting a carefully-tailored persona, and that the effect is often to 'trigger feelings of envy, misery and loneliness' in other users. 'The most common cause of Facebook frustration came from users comparing themselves socially to their peers, while the second most common source of dissatisfaction was "lack of attention" from having fewer comments, likes and general feedback compared to friends.'[24] It's another form of 'keeping up with the Joneses' – but it's far easier for the Joneses to project an aura of success and happiness online, even if in reality their lives are falling apart. Fostering this kind of dissatisfaction is at odds with the Bible's warnings about envy, and Paul's encouragement to be content in all circumstances (Philippians 4:12,13).

A key question to answer is what *kind* of engagement a platform prompts. To differing degrees they may encourage us to be passive consumers of text, images and videos, rather than actively engaging with the people behind these updates. This consumerisation of relationship can establish harmful patterns for other relationships and for our faith (see further in the chapter on consumerism: I Choose, Therefore I Am), and we may have to make a conscious decision to change the way we relate to a social network and its users to prevent that. Another issue is the requirement to monetise these platforms that has resulted from public offerings: there is now a greater incentive for companies to collect user data and host highly-targeted adverts based on personal information (see the chapter on surveillance, Chapter 6: Big Brother and privacy, Chapter 7: Keep Out!).

---

24 http://healthland.time.com/2013/01/24/why-facebook-makes-you-feel-bad-about-yourself/

DISTRACTION

At the simplest level our over-use of communications technology poses a distraction. It has been said that 'time is the currency of relationships', and this applies to all relationships, whether with God or each other. The Always-On mentality not only decreases the amount of time we have to pray, read the Bible, worship or acknowledge God's presence and hand in the world around us; it reduces the quality of those interactions when we do find time to have them. In the same way that notifications on our phones – or even the knowledge that we have unread social media updates – can interrupt or distract us from a conversation with a friend, the part of our minds that is concerned with online life can pull us away from time with God. We are not entirely present because part of us is focused elsewhere.

> *The moment of drifting into thought has been so clipped by modern technology. Our lives are filled with distraction with smartphones and all the rest. People are so locked into not being present.*
>
> GLEN HANSARD, SONGWRITER AND MUSICIAN

There is less and less time for introspection. Before the web gave us on-demand content we were more used to periods of quiet and reflection. There was still TV to watch, books to read and other distractions, but those pursuits could not be tailored to our exact desires in the same way that the infinite variety of the web offers – and were not there at our fingertips and in our pockets whenever we wanted. They also tended to require blocks of time in order to appreciate them fully, rather than being ready to fill literally every few spare seconds we experience. Few people pull out a paperback book and read another page when their friend goes to the bar to buy drinks, after all. Now we do not need to allow ourselves the time to spend with our own thoughts. Any unwanted gap in our activity can instantly be filled. The devices and technologies that give us freedom also risk enslaving us in a world of constant content and updates.

Finally, as we have explored, the Always-On culture fosters a particular mindset of busyness. The magnetic appeal of online activity and availability of content creates an expectation that it will be engaged with and consumed. Whether this activity can be considered meaningful or trivial, or a combination of the two, we fill our spare moments with it.

As so many people have found in their work lives, such activity can become a proxy for self-worth. We have a culture of long working hours. Work is so much a part of our identities that we can place an undue emphasis on it to give us a sense of meaning and a place in the world. You only need to think of the first few questions you tend to ask someone you've never met before.

The same can be true of the way we voluntarily seek out online activity. Even if it is not bad in itself, the compulsion to fill our time with it can have a corrosive impact on our identity and self-worth. It can be so easy to link our worth as a person to our levels of activity that 'wasting' time – that is, time in which we are not engaged in some overt activity – can be a reason to feel bad about ourselves. We have lost the habit of *being*, rather than *doing*.

This Always-On environment undermines our faith from two fronts. Not only does it take time away from our relationship with God, but it erodes our self-esteem in the process. Instead of seeing ourselves as creatures made in the image of and in relationship with God, it can be too easy to reduce our identity to our next online interaction.

It's clear that our remarkable access to information has the potential both to harm us and to benefit us enormously. As Christians, how do we engage with our unprecedented connectivity in a way that honours our faith and works alongside it, rather than posing an unhelpful distraction or a threat to it? One of the difficulties is that these technologies are so much a part of our lives that we rarely question them. Being more intentional about how we use them is an important first step. Some or all of the following may be helpful:

1. *Discern* the roles that connectivity and mobile devices play in your life. Checking phones and updates can easily become habitual and unthinking. Try to cultivate a mental filter and make a deliberate decision in each case: is this something necessary/desirable *right at this moment*, or could it wait until later? Is there another activity or relationship it would distract from? This could even be a face-to-face conversation we are in the middle of, a church service or quiet time. One small but practical tip is to set different alerts for different kinds of messages. For example, text messages are often used to communicate in near real-time, and you will often want to answer them quickly, whilst emails and social network updates can usually wait a while. Being able to distinguish which is which before you have interrupted what you are doing to find out how important the message is can be helpful.

2. *Practise presence*. When you are talking to someone, or praying, give that person your undivided attention. Ignore updates, and if needs be silence/turn off your

phone or computer or leave them in a different room. At mealtimes, have a 'no phone' policy so that you can be properly present for each other, without distraction or interruptions.

3. *Focus on one thing.* Multitasking sets up unhelpful mental patterns, making us less able to relate meaningfully because we are more prone to giving in to distractions. Get into the habit of doing one thing – even if it's watching TV – with your full concentration, rather than spreading your attention across two or more activities. Strange as it may seem, this is actually a long-term investment in your offline relationships. In the same way that exercising makes your body fitter, training your mind in the right way makes you better able to engage with other people. It's an odd idea that watching an episode of your favourite box set without also periodically checking your phone might make you better at relating to your friends and family – but it has some basis in reality.

4. *Start the day well.* What is the first thing you do in the morning? If it is checking your phone, as it is for most smartphone owners, think about replacing that with reading a passage of Scripture instead, or spending some time in prayer. If you charge your phone next to your bed and there's a temptation to reach for it as soon as you wake up, consider leaving it somewhere else overnight, and perhaps investing in an alarm clock.

5. *Use technology to further relationships,* not just to keep up with them. Take a little longer to connect with people, rather than just using text messages, emails and social media as a form of minimal maintenance. Use the opportunities provided by technology to strengthen your offline relationships wherever possible.

6. *Take a social media fast.* If you realise that you are spending a lot of time on social media, or it is exerting an unhealthy influence on your life, try the 30-day vacation challenge – perhaps with a group of friends as part of a conscious effort to live differently. Use the opportunity to focus on other things. Keep a record of how it affects your life, what changes, what is better and what is worse. What did you miss out on? What did you gain? Remember, too, that the essence of worship is sacrifice; this kind of fast can be a way of re-prioritising your faith.

As sacrifices go, it's hardly the same as not eating for forty days. But nevertheless, there is something oddly scary about giving up Facebook for Lent. Which is why I'm doing just that.

There are many reasons to dislike Facebook – its tax affairs, its secret psychological tests, its sometimes crass reminders of distressing life events – but they aren't what motivate my abstinence. No, it's the fact that, like millions of others, my life has become unhealthily entwined with it. It's often the first thing I see on waking, and the last thing I see before sleeping. I turn to it to settle my head after a bad dream. When I post on it – and I don't post very often – I'm far too eager to see how many likes I get. I've never considered myself especially insecure but this outlet wasn't part of our lives 10 years ago, yet it somehow seems to have become my first resort for solace and self-validation.

PETER ORMEROD IN *THE GUARDIAN*[25]

'*The first thing I see on waking, and the last thing I see before sleeping*': our Always-On culture fills not only our minds but our time. These two ideas are closely intertwined, the one being a by-product of the other, but this has particular consequences for our relationship with work – and, as importantly, for the spiritual impact on our rest.

---

25 http://www.theguardian.com/commentisfree/2016/feb/08/giving-up-facebook-lent-online-self

3. WORK AND REST

HOW WE USE TIME-SAVING TECHNOLOGIES – ALL THE TIME

I've freelanced for years, and I've always found it hard to maintain a work/life balance. The problem with freelance work is that there's either too much or not enough. When you're starting out, you have to work hard to establish a reputation as someone diligent and reliable, who will turn out good material consistently and respond quickly to requests. That means you have to think very hard about turning down work – unless you've already established a good relationship, you might not get another opportunity with that client. If several people ask you for work at the same time, well, that's a few late nights and/or early mornings.

When you're working with companies in the same country, you can expect that to happen occasionally. But at least the requests generally come in during office hours. A couple of years back, though, my client base changed dramatically. I started working in a new sector of the technology industry, with people all over the world. It was fast-moving and exciting – like working for a start-up, helping different organisations and individuals communicate totally new ideas. In any given day I might be working with people in America, Europe and Australia – and a few in locations I never discovered. Many of them didn't keep regular hours either. The upshot was that I was fielding emails and Skype and Slack conversations around the clock. First thing in the morning and last thing at night, there would be new messages to read.

I could have and probably should have put some rules in place about when I read and replied to work messages, but the freelancer mentality dies hard. When you've spent years chasing the next piece of work (in between periods of wondering how you're possibly going to get everything done on time) you can get pretty bad at saying 'no'.

Over the next few months I learned what plenty of other people have: that constantly keeping up with the feed of information – whether that's work messages or status updates or new pictures of humorously-posed cats – isn't good for you. It changes the way you think. With a young baby in the house, sleep was already disturbed. Now, whenever I was woken up, the temptation was always to check in with work, find out what was coming down the track and get a head start on the day. After all, I was already tired, I had a lot to do and didn't know how much more I'd be offered in the coming week, so it made sense to 'bank' time, right? As a knowledge worker, someone involved in communicating ideas, I didn't always need to be in front of a computer to do that; I just needed to be able to think. Pretty soon the pattern was established: if I was awake, I was working.

The last chapter explored one downside of the communications technologies that facilitate the amazing levels of connectivity we routinely use and enjoy: adopted uncritically, they actually prevent us from connecting properly with each other. The constant stream of information fills our consciousness, all too often posing an unhelpful distraction from something more important.

As well as headspace, there's the other reality that we touched on in the last chapter: our time is limited. We might be connected 24/7, but there are still only 24 hours in a day and 7 days a week.

We're using more and more of that time online, whether for work or recreational purposes.

It's strange that many of us spend all day staring at screens in the course of our paid employment, then come home and stare at a screen for a few more hours to unwind. Government surveys suggest the average American watches five hours of TV a day (a lot more for older people, less for younger ones).[26] A thirty-year-old American working eight hours a day still manages to find time for four hours of TV, albeit including weekend viewing.

WORK AND REST IN THE ALWAYS-ON CULTURE

Not that there is a clear line between home and work anymore. One of the most simultaneously fantastic and insidiously corrosive effects of the information revolution has been the ability to work from anywhere and at any time (as I've discovered to my own benefit and cost). Mobile technology means that it has never been easier to keep up with our paid jobs outside of office hours. The office doesn't even have to be an office. It can be a coffee shop, a train, five spare minutes waiting in a queue – or at home. And it's not just a question of accessing work emails from our personal devices, in the evenings or at the weekends. It's the fact that work barely *has* defined hours any more. Work follows us around on our mobile devices and computers. Even shift workers may have to keep up with administration outside of their set hours.

We might still keep nominal fixed office hours, but we don't work nine-to-five any more (especially in the city – though, to give Dolly Parton her due, it's still enough to drive you crazy if you let it).[27] For many entrepreneurs and freelancers, the concept of

---

26 http://www.nydailynews.com/life-style/average-american-watches-5-hours-tv-day-article-1.1711954
27 https://en.wikipedia.org/wiki/9_to_5_(Dolly_Parton_song).

'normal' work hours is almost entirely meaningless, a throwback to a different time when work had to be done in fixed places and mutually convenient times. We don't even do weekends in the way we used to, because it's just as easy to answer an email on a Saturday or Sunday as it is any other day – and it can seem useful to spend those 'extra' hours to get ahead on the next week or catch up on the last.

> In 2015, the number of emails sent and received per day total over 205 billion. This figure is expected to grow at an average annual rate of 3% over the next four years, reaching over 246 billion by the end of 2019 ... In 2015, the number of business emails sent and received per user per day totals 122 emails per day. This figure continues to show growth and is expected to average 126 messages sent and received per business user by the end of 2019.[28]

Is it really so bad to take a few minutes to answer an email, or an hour or two of our own leisure time to write up a report for a meeting? On the surface of it, few of us might think so. Hard work, diligence and productivity are laudable, and few success stories are built on laziness. But perhaps strangely – to our minds, at least – the Bible has a lot to say about rest. Despite the numerous warnings to sluggards in Proverbs (6:6–8, 9–11; 13:4; 26:13–16 ...), *stopping* work at the right time was considered even more important. For one day a week, from sunset on Friday to sunset on Saturday, everyone had to take a break. The principle was so central to Israelite life that it found its way into the Ten Commandments, alongside idolatry, theft and murder. Clearly, God views rest as a very different priority than we typically do.

Neither is this solely relevant to one day a week. The Bible's teaching on the Sabbath extends to the broader rhythms of life, work

---

28 http://www.radicati.com/wp/wp-content/uploads/2015/02/Email-Statistics-Report-2015-2019-Executive-Summary.pdf

and rest. It places 'rest' in the category of religious observance: rest is not just a gift to us, or something we can take or leave depending on whether it is convenient to us. It is part of our worship – a surprising and challenging idea we'll explore in more detail below.

Even before we start to unpack any spiritual consequences, though, it's clear that these trends have serious impacts on their own terms. Businesses naturally want their employees to be productive, and being able to respond quickly to emails and new developments is part of what helps them stay competitive. Unfortunately, a growing body of research shows that in chasing that productivity they are undermining their own success. Work-related stress, depression and anxiety cost UK businesses ten million work days per year – and absences due to mental health issues are rising sharply. One of the major causes of increased stress, anxiety and depression is our inability to disconnect from work.

> In an age of connected technology 24/7, phone alerts, texts, emails, status updates, posts and tweets, during and outside working hours, employees increasingly feel unable to switch off. The concept of the 'working holiday' has entered the modern vernacular, due to the availability of remote working coupled with job insecurity fears.[29]

In other words, working more hours has proven to be a false economy. We have not taken on board the maxim to work smarter rather than harder. Meanwhile, our time in work is less efficient due to the distractions posed by social media and the web. Estimates vary, but studies suggest the average employee spends around a quarter of their work time on unproductive online activities, including an hour on social media (Facebook and LinkedIn being the most common choices – it seems employees spend a lot of

---

29 http://www.cipd.co.uk/pm/peoplemanagement/b/weblog/archive/2015/11/26/employers-have-a-duty-to-deal-with-stress-and-mental-health-at-work.aspx

time at work looking for a new job). Whilst some companies try to prevent their people from logging in to time-wasting sites, many use social media for their own business engagement – and most employees can, in any case, circumvent the restrictions by using their own devices.

It is almost as if we're only really working the same amount that we were before, just spreading out those productive hours over a longer period of time – to the detriment of both work and leisure.

REST IN THE BIBLE

Our use of communications technology and the blurred lines it creates between work and the rest of life is highly relevant to how we approach time away from the office or 'work' in general, and particularly our weekly shared day off (generally Sunday, for most of us nowadays, rather than the biblical Sabbath[30]). So why is the Bible so keen on a weekly day of rest? For that matter, what *is* rest?

Like so many other aspects of Israelite life and law, the importance of the Sabbath reflects the misery of the Israelites' lives in Egypt.

> *They put slave masters over them to oppress them with forced labour, and they built Pithom and Rameses as store cities for Pharaoh. But the more they were oppressed, the more they multiplied and spread; so the Egyptians came to dread the Israelites and worked them ruthlessly. They made their lives bitter with harsh labour in brick and mortar and with all kinds of work in the fields; in all their harsh labour the Egyptians worked them ruthlessly.*

EXODUS 1:11–14

30 The Christian day of rest probably moved from the Jewish Sabbath to the first day of the week (Sunday) as early as the second century.

And so, when God delivered the Israelites from Pharaoh, he gave them laws to ensure that their own nation – the one they would build for themselves in a new land, free from Pharaoh's tyranny – would be established upon very different principles. The Not Like Egypt aspect of Israel extended to almost every aspect of life: the way their economy operated, their model of kingship and government, their treatment of slaves and captives, even the way they divided up their time.

> *I am the LORD your God, who brought you out of Egypt, out of the land of slavery … Observe the Sabbath day by keeping it holy, as the LORD your God has commanded you. Six days you shall labour and do all your work, but the seventh day is a Sabbath to the LORD your God. On it you shall not do any work, neither you, nor your son or daughter, nor your male or female servant, nor your ox, your donkey or any of your animals, nor any foreigner residing in your towns, so that your male and female servants may rest, as you do. Remember that you were slaves in Egypt and that the LORD your God brought you out of there with a mighty hand and an outstretched arm. Therefore the LORD your God has commanded you to observe the Sabbath day.*

DEUTERONOMY 5:6, 12–15

The Sabbath was incredibly important for the Israelites. To us, a weekly day off from work might represent little more than a welcome break and a chance to attend church and spend time with friends and family. But we rarely treat it so seriously that we avoid *all* forms of work, whatever that might mean. In the Bible, though, in common with most of the other Ten Commandments, the Sabbath was considered so sacrosanct that working on it was punishable by death.

While the Israelites were in the wilderness, a man was found gathering wood on the Sabbath day. Those who found him gathering wood brought him to Moses and Aaron and the whole assembly, and they kept him in custody, because it was not clear what should be done to him. Then the LORD said to Moses, 'The man must die. The whole assembly must stone him outside the camp.' So the assembly took him outside the camp and stoned him to death, as the LORD commanded Moses.

NUMBERS 15:32–36

This is a huge challenge to us today. Whilst the death penalty isn't something we would want to transfer to our treatment of work and rest, it does signal just how important this issue was (and presumably remains) to God.

So why was the Sabbath taken so seriously? It turns out that there are a number of reasons, reflecting the importance of the Sabbath not just as a day of rest but as a mechanism built into the life of the Israelites' community and constituting a key element of their religious identity and system of justice.

Resting on the Sabbath was not just a personal matter intended to give individuals a break from work, as we often consider it. As well as being forbidden from working, the Israelites were not allowed to require anyone *else* to work, either. *Everyone* was to rest, regardless of whether they were a native Israelite or foreigner. Even animals were not to be made to work. 'On it you shall not do any work, neither you, nor your son or daughter, nor your male or female servant, nor your ox, your donkey or any of your animals, nor any foreigner residing in your towns ...'

Farming would be the most obvious form of work to the Israelites, but other forms of 'work' were clearly included in the ban on working on the Sabbath. The story of the man found collecting wood shows that even those tasks necessary for day-to-day life should be avoided for a day. In Exodus 16, God provides manna on six days of the week, and instructs the Israelites to gather twice as much on the sixth day, so they could rest on the Sabbath (Exodus 16:21–23, 29–30).

By the time of the New Testament, the rabbis had interpreted the ban on Sabbath work in minute detail, as one story from the Talmud illustrates: 'R. Judah b. Habiba recited: We may not prepare strong salt water. What is strong salt water? – Rabbah and R. Joseph b. Abba both say: Such that an egg floats in it.'[31] When the disciples picked grain to eat the Pharisees complained they were breaking the Sabbath (Mark 2:23–28). Even non-essential healing was forbidden on the Sabbath – an idea Jesus firmly opposed.[32]

Even in the Old Testament, the ban applied to any kind of economic activity, not just physical work. The prophet Amos criticises merchants for impatiently waiting out the Sabbath, so that they could get back to their dishonest practices.

> Hear this, you who trample the needy and do away with the poor of the land, saying, 'When will the New Moon be over that we may sell grain, and the Sabbath be ended that we may market wheat?' – skimping on the measure, boosting the price and cheating with dishonest scales, buying the poor with silver and the needy for a pair of sandals, selling even the sweepings with the wheat.

AMOS 8:4–6

Amos' words point to a principle that has never been more relevant than it is for us today, in our hyper-connected and work-obsessed culture. The day of rest isn't just about our individual convenience and enjoyment. It's not a consumer choice, to be accepted or refused depending on the pressures of life and personal whim. It is about something far, far more profound.

---

31 Talmud Shabbat 108b.
32 See Mark 3:1–5 and Matthew 12:11–12.

The Sabbath was a hallmark of the Israelites. It was not simply a weekly holiday. It was a part of their core identity as the people of God. The Sabbath was God's reminder that he had brought them out of Egypt, a land of harsh slavery and constant work. The Egyptian calendar was not divided into weeks, and records suggest there were no days of rest for most workers. One of the key reasons that breaking the Sabbath was deemed so serious was because it indicated a trivialisation of God's grace. '"Sabbath-gathering" reflects a desire to return to the economic conditions associated with Pharaoh's rule and thus signifies the rejection of YHWH's lordship.'[33] Working on the Sabbath was tantamount to idolatry.

This matches well with Amos' criticism of the merchants who hated the enforced weekly break from trading. These people had prioritised making money over everything else, including pausing to acknowledge God's grace in rescuing them from Egypt. They had made money and commerce into an idol, and it is little wonder that this mentality went hand-in-hand with injustice since they would do anything to pursue it.

The New Testament does not fundamentally change the approach to the Sabbath. Rather than abolishing the Law, Jesus completes it (Matthew 5:17). The *principle* of Sabbath rest was and remains sound, but its expression by some of the religious authorities of the day had the effect of undermining its ultimate purpose. Superficial and unthinking Sabbath observance ended up harming others, not blessing them, as God intended.

So the Sabbath was a chance to rest from work, something the Israelites had not been permitted to do in Egypt, and to worship God and to spend time with their families and communities. The regular religious festivals served the same purpose, bringing the people together to remember their history and to reinforce their

---

33 Jonathan Burnside, '"What Shall We Do With The Sabbath-Gatherer?" A Narrative Approach to a "Hard Case" in Biblical Law (Numbers 15:32–26)'. *Vetus Testamentum* 60 (2010), pp. 45–62. See online at http://seekjustice. co.uk/GJSteachingresources/sabbath_Bible_biblical_law.pdf

identity. Although the rabbis carried the principle to extremes in their detailed rules about Sabbath observance, the intention was to honour God (even if the reality was sometimes a distracting mess of regulations that followed the letter but not the spirit of the law).[34]

WHAT IS 'WORK' ANYWAY?

In New Testament times, the rabbis expanded the biblical verses on the Sabbath into large and complex bodies of teaching that, as Jesus commented, missed the point about what they were supposed to achieve in the first place. For us, as for the Israelites, there is the nagging question of what we should consider 'work'.

Given the purposes of the biblical Sabbath, and the effect that the Always-On culture has on us, there's a strong case for suggesting that we should not just be resting from our formal, paid work, but from some of the wider practices that connectivity encourages in us. The average user checks their smartphone 150 times a day and spends upwards of three hours using their phones. The majority of these instances may not be for work (and may be a distraction *at* work, which is another issue). Their purpose may even be to connect with other people through social media and text messages. But instead of being deliberate, considered actions, many of these checks are little more than involuntary tics or a way of filling a few spare moments.

Ultimately, the purpose of the Sabbath is, as Jesus said, to do good, not evil, and to save life, not to kill (Mark 3:4). When we reduce rest to no more than physical inactivity or a break from paid work, we miss this point. Our lives are full of screen-time, at work or voluntarily in the rest of our days. Computers and mobile devices have become woven into everything we do. Whilst in many instances this has a positive effect, allowing us to connect with

---

34 See Matthew 23.

people and maintain relationships, in other cases it distances and distracts us from other people. The worst part of it is that we rarely question what the effect will be, because picking up our phones has become such an involuntary part of our lives.

Perhaps, like the Israelites who struggled with the idea of rest after so long in Egypt, work and work-like activities have become so normal to us that we can no longer discern what 'work' really is any more. 'I will not be mastered by anything', writes Paul[35] but we readily give up by choice the freedom granted to us in grace and the rest required from us as a part of our worship.

The Always-On culture has the predictable downside that it becomes very hard to switch off. We get into the habit of being able to keep up with emails and updates, whether for work or leisure, until it becomes almost reflexive – eating our time without our conscious permission. The Bible's teaching highlights that rest does not just mean a break from paid work. Neither is 'rest' simply inactivity or another leisure pursuit we can take or leave. It is a form of worship, an expression of gratitude for God's grace in delivering us from slavery. It is also a corporate activity, meaning that we should spend our weekly day off in ways that support our friendships and family, and relationships within our community of faith. For Christians, reclaiming this element of our worship and gratitude must be a priority.

1. *Rethink rest*, understanding it both as a part of worship and as a gift God has given you to enjoy, whether that is on a weekly day off or at intervals throughout the day.

---

35   1 Corinthians 6:12.

Take time away from computers and phones, unless there is a specific (and good) reason to use them.

2. *Reclaim the day of rest as a hallmark of Christian faith*, just as the Sabbath was and remains a hallmark of Jewish religious observance. Set aside distractions and make sure you spend time deepening key relationships, whether that means meeting face-to-face or whether it involves using technology – so long as that is a conscious decision. Eating together is often a good way of spending quality time with people, but make these meals a phone-free time!

3. *Enforce rest at your workplace.* If you are a business leader, cultivate a culture of rest outside of office hours, wherever possible. At the same time, ensure you have a clear policy of what constitutes acceptable internet practice at work. Whether or not you are in charge, do everything you reasonably can to enable yourself and others to disconnect from work outside of office hours. For example, you could make it clear that any emails or non-essential messages sent to colleagues late in the afternoon do not need a response until the next day.

4. *No working vacations.* If the purpose of the Sabbath was to rest, not just for rest's sake but as a way of honouring God and connecting with other people, this is something we should bear in mind throughout the year. The Israelites celebrated several annual festivals, involving longer periods of time. When you take a holiday, make sure it really is a holiday!

5. *Carve out regular time for God.* The Israelites' days were punctuated with actions of thanks and worship. Deuteronomy 6 instructs the Israelites: 'These com-mandments that I give you today are to be on your

hearts. Impress them on your children. Talk about them when you sit at home and when you walk along the road, when you lie down and when you get up. Tie them as symbols on your hands and bind them on your foreheads. Write them on the doorframes of your houses and on your gates' (Deuteronomy 6:6–9). Even if this was not meant literally, it is an encouragement to meditate on God's commands at regular intervals through the day when we have spare time. Modern equivalents might be a daily commute, mealtimes together, or quiet periods before going to bed – time that we often now spend on our phones and computers, as if we must squeeze out every last minute of the day in online activity.

6. *Plan your time to make sure you have time.* The nature of Always-On life means we can do things on a far more ad hoc basis than we used to. However, the ability to complete tasks at any time and anywhere just as often means we leave them until the last minute. This 'just in time' mentality extends to everything from planning get-togethers with friends to Christmas shopping online. This can result in additional stress and lost/wasted time – especially if the technology on which we rely happens not to work, as, for example, when everyone is trying to pay for their car tax at the same time.[36]

---

36 'Thousands unable to renew car tax, as new system stalls', http://www.bbc.co.uk/news/business-29430979

What would happen if you lost your phone? Would it
be little more than an inconvenience, or something much,
much worse?
Many of us have our lives tied to our phones. We access social
networking and email from them, and have them logged into
our accounts all the time. That email address is probably the
form of verification we use to sign up to new services and
confirm changes to existing ones. Chances are there's a lot
of personal information buried in old emails, text messages,
social networking profiles and other accounts, all accessible
to anyone who has your device. Birthdays, place of birth,
mother's maiden name, passwords, bank account details –
just about everything. There's a good chance you haven't
even password protected it; around a third of us haven't
even bothered to set a four-digit lock code, let alone activate
settings that encrypt your data or enable you to find the
device if it is lost.[37] That's an open door to anyone who gets
their hands on your phone.
An unsecured phone is a goldmine for cyber criminals
who can profit handsomely from identity theft. But there's
another question surrounding identity when it comes to your
smartphone. When your identity is so bound up with your
device and your online profiles, who are you without them?
And perhaps more to the point – who are you with them?

---

37   http://www.cnbc.com/2014/04/26/most-americans-dont-secure-their-
     smartphones.html

4. WHO ARE YOU?

HOW DO YOU KNOW THAT WHAT YOU SEE IS WHAT YOU GET?

'Good morning sir, I am calling from ********. We've had reports that your area has been experiencing slow internet speeds.' The person claiming to be from my Internet Service Provider was obviously based in a call centre somewhere in India, but since outsourcing is perfectly normal and I had indeed been experiencing slow internet speeds, I decided it was worth seeing where things went.

'Firstly, sir, I'd like you to open a command prompt.' The caller took me through a number of steps to display my computer's CLSID – what she described as a unique identifier that she could use to prove she really was from my ISP and was monitoring my computer. She read out the number, which did indeed match. 'Great, so now we can proceed.' I would need to download a small piece of software to fix the problem, she said, and started to give me the URL.

Pretty convincing so far, but it's never worth letting these things go unchallenged. Whilst we were talking I did a quick internet search for 'CLSID' and soon found that it wasn't unique at all. It's a rather obscure identifier in the Windows Registry – part of the operating system that no regular user ever needs to go looking around in. Banking on the fact that 99 per cent of people wouldn't have a clue what it was, the caller was using it as a short-cut to gain my trust.

At that point I confronted her and the call soon ended. Had I continued, I would have downloaded the 'fix', which was in reality ransomware – a piece of software that would have locked my computer and prevented me from using it until I had paid a fee to have it unlocked. If you don't pay up, you can expect to lose everything on your computer and have to start from scratch. Work files, photos, music, anything you haven't backed up is gone. Variations on the theme involve the scammers convincing you to let them take control of your computer to rid it of malware or virus infections (which you don't have), or updating security or ownership certificates (which you don't need), and then charging you for it.

As these things go it was a pretty sophisticated scam. The caller knew my ISP company, and she didn't try to ask for passwords or for direct payments. All she was asking was for me to download a piece of software to fix a problem (albeit only one she'd identified by chance – it turns out that slow internet speeds is just something my ISP provides routinely, for no extra charge). How many people would have fallen for it? Plenty, if the warnings on the web are anything to go by. It's a common and very expensive scam.

And what might the practical and spiritual consequences have been? There's the lost time already spent talking on the phone, and potentially hours afterwards fixing my computer, that I would have preferred to spend with my wife and children, relaxing or doing more useful things that particular Saturday morning. The anger, frustration, resentment and distraction that come from being caught out and that would almost inevitably overflow into other areas of life, detracting from my relationships with God and other people. The money that I might have been tempted to pay (typically up to £200) to make the problem go away, which I could have spent on much more worthwhile things. The increased cynicism and suspicion I'd be left to deal with. If it had been a work or church computer, there would have been a whole other set of consequences, affecting many different people.

Always-On means that we have access to all the information we want. The flipside of this is the distractions it brings and the impact it has on headspace: it's hard for us to switch off. It means we can work or complete important tasks at any time – and conversely that we end up doing these things *all* the time. Of course, it's possible to enjoy the benefits without suffering the downsides, but managing that in practice isn't as easy as we might think it should be.

But there's another subtle message the Always-On culture sends. You're always connected, but the right time to use it is *now*. You can check for new updates now, so you should. You can answer that email at 10pm, so you should. You can text one friend while talking to another in person. You can break off a face-to-face conversation because your phone is buzzing. You can catch up on work or do some shopping on Sunday. The web is a great enabler – in both senses of the word. It brings access to all kinds of useful activities, and it's an enabler in the sense that it facilitates addiction, compulsive behaviours and harmful habits. It's the digital equivalent of a mate encouraging you to have another drink when it's already time to go home. Go on, click this, answer this, download that. Returning to the theme of power and who's in charge – it's clear it's not always us.

There is something about the opportunities that connectivity brings that can easily bypass our critical faculties. We can be unquestioning users. We put a lot of information online. Status updates about what we're doing. Phone numbers, email and contact details. Photographs of ourselves, our nearest and dearest. Celebrity hacking scandals involving nude photos haven't dissuaded the rest of us from uploading more mainstream photos, whether to social media or to cloud storage. Our precise location at any given time, supplied by our device's built-in GPS. We sign up for new services with a couple of taps or clicks. We don't read the Terms and Conditions. We reuse passwords. We trust the experts and the platforms we use, ignoring the risks, even though we've heard countless examples of identity theft, lost data, fraud, stalking and harassment. Tacitly, we think: 'It won't happen to me.' We don't think before we click. We let go of responsibility and give power away freely. In short, we *trust*.

WHAT YOU SEE IS WHAT YOU GET (WYSIWYG)

Back in the early days of word processing software, user interfaces were often rudimentary and relied on the editor including symbols and code to set the layout of the text. What appeared on the screen was nothing like what emerged from the printer. As the software progressed, new graphical interfaces were created that showed the final layout of the document on the screen. These were marketed as 'WYSIWYG' (What You See Is What You Get) editors, which we now take for granted. WYSIWYG reflected the frustration and inconvenience of seeing one thing on the screen but quite another in real life.

The Always-On mentality raises the key question of who you are interacting with online. Because, just like early text-based editing software, what people show you online is not what you get in real life.

Often this happens through no real fault of their or our own. As we explored in the previous chapter, relationships online are usually thinner. We may have hundreds of 'friends' online, but only a handful of people we relate to more deeply in real life. We don't have the time to maintain meaningful relationships with all of our online connections. Moreover, there's lots of information about them we don't have access to online, including the way they relate to other people (Multiplexity). What that means is that you only really get an 'edited' version of someone online, at best. It's inevitable. At worst, the person you are communicating with online is someone completely different to the one they present to you, as in the story of the CLSID scammer at the beginning of this chapter – or in the well-known episode of Amina Abdallah, reported across the media in 2011.

Amina Abdallah Arraf al Omari was a Syrian-American blogger who posted regularly on her blog, A Gay Girl in Damascus. As a self-identifying lesbian in a repressive regime hostile towards LGBT minorities, Aminah wrote regularly about Middle Eastern politics, Syrian culture, sexuality and gender. The blog gained popularity and her photo became one of the public faces of the opposition in the Syrian pro-democracy movement in 2011. Major news outlets published interviews with her, conducted over email, though she was prevented from meeting reporters in person due to harassment by the Syrian secret police. Finally, in June 2011, Amina's cousin posted that she had been kidnapped by three armed men, leading to widespread condemnation.

Mainstream media outlets reported the abduction, but critics increasingly started to ask whether Amina Abdallah had been a fake all along. None of the details of the accounts could be confirmed. Emails from 'Amina' were traced back to a computer in Edinburgh. The photo turned out to be that of a Croatian living in London, which had been copied from Facebook. Finally, an American postgraduate student, Tom MacMaster, admitted to being the real author. MacMaster claimed that the fictional character of Amina gave him greater authority in expressing his views on the Middle East, and that he would not have been taken seriously if his readers had known he was a 40-year-old male American graduate student. News outlets were forced to publish apologies over the convincing hoax, which was decried as 'indefensible', 'narcissistic', 'arrogant fantasy', and even described as a case of the newly-coined disorder, 'Munchausen by Internet'.

When relationships are Direct[38] – present, face to face, WYSIWYG – it's a lot easier to know someone more fully. When the relationship is mediated to some extent by technology, such as is the case with most relationships online, it becomes a lot harder to gather all the information to learn what you need to know about someone. There is something in particular about social media that draws out particular character traits, with impacts both for others online and for our own identities. 'Even subtler, perhaps, is the way that information technology elicits and emphasises certain aspects of self, especially articulation and assertiveness. While these are not necessarily undesirable in themselves, we might also ask how the fruit of the Spirit will be evident in email communication and chatrooms. How will gentleness and self-control – more often evidenced by presence or action or even silence – be made visible here? Our communication technologies create a climate that favours different fruit.'[39]

This is not to say that online relationships are not or cannot be genuine and meaningful. Online communities, facilitated by forums and instant messaging, provide many of the same purposes as offline communities – and for various reasons may do so better than in real life. The dispersed nature of virtual communities means there is always likely to be someone online, and messages usually receive a fast response. Although communities are based on a particular common interest, discussion is generally far broader in scope and they can serve purposes far beyond the immediate

---

38 See 'Relational Proximity' in Schluter and Lee, *The R Factor* (Hodder & Stoughton, 1993). The authors identify five 'dimensions of relational proximity': characteristics that facilitate the building of close relationships. These are Directness (unmediated communication), Continuity (shared time together over the long term), Multiplexity (broader background information about that person), Parity (a healthy dynamic of power) and Commonality (shared aims).

39 David Pullinger, 'The Impact of Information Technology on Personal Identity' (The Bible in Transmission, 2003), see https://www.biblesociety. org.uk/uploads/content/bible_in_transmission/files/2003_summer/BiT_ Summer_2003_Pullinger.pdf

reason for joining. There is often a significant degree of emotional and even practical support (see the example at the end of the chapter on privacy, Keep Out!). People may or may not go on to meet offline, and they may form long-lasting relationships of various kinds – friendships, romantic relationships and business partnerships, to name a few.

However, as we've seen, the nature of the web means online relationships can be prone to abuse. There's something about the *ability* to communicate freely with anyone online that often short-circuits or steamrollers our suspicions. It's so *easy* – just a few clicks or taps on a touchscreen – that we just do. And this, like everything else we do online or offline, has both a spiritual dimension and consequences in the real world.

At the extreme end there are the horror stories that we have all seen and heard on the news. The high-profile cases of online grooming, child sexual abuse and murder that have become all too familiar. The sixfold rise in first-date rape claims linked to online dating apps over the last five years – likely only the tip of the iceberg.[40] The fact that almost 80 per cent of children aged 10 to 12 have social media accounts, despite being below the official age limit;[41] that a significant proportion of these have experienced online bullying and almost half have connections they have never met in real life.[42]

Then there are the hacks, scams and identity thefts that are routine if we slip up or forget to maintain best practice online. Harvesting passwords and gaining fraudulent access to email and social media accounts now constitutes an entire industry of its own, carried out indiscriminately by automated networks of 'zombie' computers. (If it hasn't happened to you yet, it's probably because you're unusually careful or lucky.)

---

40 http://www.bbc.co.uk/news/uk-35513052
41 http://www.bbc.co.uk/news/education-35524429
42 http://www.pewinternet.org/2015/07/16/concerns-about-children-social-media-and-technology-use/

We'll be looking further at some of these ideas in the chapters on surveillance and privacy (chapters 6 and 7). For now, we can say that the anonymity of the web places a question over our online interactions, whether that involves downloading an app, replying to an email or talking to someone online. When we do that, we are trusting the person or people at the other end of the interaction, and in doing so we are giving them power over us. It may not feel like it at the time – after all, the activity itself might be as quick and easy as clicking a link – but with hindsight it can often become clear that is what has happened. It can cost us time, money, our ability to take decisions that affect our own lives. When we give over control, we potentially give over part of our freedom, too. That's not something we should do lightly.

WHO AM I?

There's another side to the anonymity of online interactions. It's not just other people who might be misrepresenting themselves. I can be someone else online too. I might not create a totally new online persona (though plenty of people do), but I can edit myself. Of all the information I upload about myself, I can tailor what other people see to give the impression I want. I can present the best side of my personality – the happiest events, the funniest comments, the most jealousy-inducing photographs on social media. Probably all of us are guilty of this online self-censorship to some extent or other.

In other instances, it's necessary and desirable to reveal only a part of yourself online. For example, if you have a social media presence for your work, it would not be appropriate to share the same information you might with close friends with colleagues and customers. This is not disingenuous; it is simply what goes on in real life. Not all relationships are the same, and different relationships entail different roles. A close friend might know where we live, how many children we have and what they look like; sharing this information with a transient customer we have never met before is another matter. Many professionals start to run into problems when those they work with start to request connections with them on social media – such as pupils asking to 'friend' a teacher. The content and connections of a LinkedIn account, geared towards business connections, might be very different to those of a personal Facebook account.

There are other implications to being too public online. If we disclose too much information, we may be the victims of identity theft. Moreover, as we will explore further in the chapters on privacy and surveillance, giving away personal information has an impact on our freedom because it gives other people power over us. When signing up for certain services, there is sometimes a legitimate case for using throwaway email addresses and usernames, especially if we don't know what the host company will do with them. In many instances, these details will be sold on to third parties, used to track our online behaviour in some way, or simply stored insecurely and vulnerable to exploit by hackers. Whistle-blowers rely on their anonymity to stay safe.

There is always, however, the question of integrity. Selective disclosure, necessary and important though it is, brings the opportunity of presenting yourself as someone very different to the person you are in real life. Many forums and social networks don't require a real name at all, and internet culture is frequently to use a nickname or handle that has no link with your real identity. Often there are good reasons for this, and anonymity (or pseudonymity) is not innately bad or misleading. But the thinner the relationships permitted by the medium, the more scope there is to misrepresent yourself, intentionally or otherwise. The so-called online disinhibition effect is strong.

We cannot present ourselves online with the full 'bandwidth' or richness of a relationship as experienced in real life, between friends who know each other in many contexts. (It is worth noting, of course, that we tend to edit our real-life personas in different relationships, too – it's just that it's much, much easier to do it online.) Nevertheless, the results of this PR exercise lie somewhere on a spectrum from light censorship to outright and systematic lying. This censorship extends to how we engage with others' ideas and identities. Different communities have established online etiquette and there is very often the tacit understanding that everyone will conform to accepted – if unstated – norms. The equivalent situation of course again occurs in real life, but the online version is usually more intense. This can result in a kind of collusion not to question anything, despite knowing it to be false. The presentation of the 'perfect life' is admired, even if we know it is not a reality. Dishonest or misleading comments are left unchallenged. Standards of conduct and communication are adhered to rigorously; if a reply is left too long it may be taken as a personal insult or a lack of interest. And, of course, if the lack of conformity reaches unacceptable levels, there is always the ultimate sanction: the passive-aggressive 'unfriend' or 'ignore'.

IDENTITY, ANONYMITY AND INTEGRITY IN THE BIBLE

There are plenty of examples of biblical characters who choose to remain anonymous for one reason or another – some with deception and harm in mind, others for more benign purposes. When God appears to Abraham, he does so in the form of a human visitor (Genesis 18:1–15). Jacob wrestled with a man, only later discovering that it was God (Genesis 32:22–32). And there are many occasions in the gospels – for different reasons – where Jesus does not want his identity to be publicly known.

One of the clearest examples of real anonymity in the Bible is provided by Jesus after the resurrection. In John 20, Mary Magdalene stays in front of the empty tomb after Peter and John have left. Jesus then appears to her but she does not recognise him at first. 'Thinking he was the gardener, she said, "Sir, if you have carried him away, tell me where you have put him, and I will get him." Jesus said to her, "Mary." She turned towards him and cried out in Aramaic, "Rabboni!" (which means "Teacher")' (John 20:15–16).

It is only after Jesus speaks to her that she understands who it is. Perhaps she simply didn't recognise him – perhaps she was distracted by grief, or she didn't see him because he was quite literally the last person she expected to see walking around there at the time. But anonymity or mistaken identity appears to be a running theme of the post-resurrection appearances.

In the Emmaus Road account in Luke's gospel (24:13–35), Jesus' true identity is deliberately hidden from the two disciples who meet him. 'Now that same day two of them were going to a village called Emmaus, about seven miles from Jerusalem. They were talking with each other about everything that had happened. As they talked and discussed these things with each other, Jesus himself came up and walked along with them; but *they were kept from recognising him*' (Luke 24:13–15, italics mine). The parallel version in Mark 16 says, 'Afterwards Jesus appeared in a different form to two of them while they were walking in the country' (Mark 16:12). In John 21, the disciples do not recognise Jesus from either his appearance (at a distance) or his voice. It is only when he tells them to throw the net out on the other side of the boat and they catch a miraculously large number of fish that John realises who it is on the shore (John 21:7). Paul writes that the resurrection body will be different from our physical body; the seed that is planted looks nothing like the wheat that eventually grows from it (1 Corinthians 15:35–44). Perhaps this was the case with Jesus.

Whatever the explanation, Jesus' identity was intentionally hidden on at least one occasion and possibly more. In Luke, Jesus uses his anonymity as a teaching opportunity. The two disciples learn things through discussion and wrestling with their own confusion that they would not if Jesus simply appeared to them. The disciple Thomas later requires incontrovertible proof: 'Unless I see the nail marks in his hands and put my finger where the nails were, and put my hand into his side, I will not believe it' (John 20:25). But, says Jesus, 'Because you have seen me, you have believed; blessed are those who have not seen and yet have believed' (John 20:29). It seems that Jesus' disguised appearance is a device to instil greater faith in those who meet him.

There are other occasions on which biblical authors and characters are referenced obliquely or anonymously. In 2 Corinthians 12:1–10, Paul writes, 'I know a man in Christ who fourteen years ago was caught up to the third heaven ... I will boast about a man like that, but I will not boast about myself, except about my weaknesses.' Commentators generally agree that Paul is writing about himself here. Presumably this episode would be known to those closest to him, but not necessarily to wider audiences. In Mark 14:51–52, there is the account of a young man who is present at the arrest of Jesus and manages to escape the guards. 'When they seized him, he fled naked, leaving his garment behind.' This is likely to be one of the disciples or Jesus' other close followers. Because the reference only appears in Mark, many critics believe it was the author of Mark's gospel himself (John Mark). Because he was implicated in the arrest, it could be dangerous to be identified by name. It may also be that, like Paul, he wanted to display humility rather than boast about his presence at this key event in the gospel story. Humility is also the reason that we are commanded to give anonymously (Matthew 6:1–4). 'Then your Father, who sees what is done in secret, will reward you.'

Of course, online there are many occasions on which the reasons for anonymity might not be so benign, and the same is true in the Bible. Rebekah helps Jacob disguise himself so he can trick Isaac into giving him Esau's birthright (Genesis 27:1–40). Saul hides his identity so he can consult a witch (having previously banned all mediums and spiritists) because he did not receive an answer from the Lord about the outcome of a battle (1 Samuel 28). And there is this warning from Paul, 'For such people are false apostles, deceitful workers, masquerading as apostles of Christ. And no wonder, for Satan himself masquerades as an angel of light. It is not surprising, then, if his servants also masquerade as servants of righteousness. Their end will be what their actions deserve' (2 Corinthians 11:13–15).

Anonymity in itself is not wrong. What appears to matter more are the *reasons and motives* for anonymity. For Jesus, his disguised identity seems to lead to a deeper faith on the part of the disciples. Anonymous giving is supposed to be the norm. In other cases, such as Saul and the Witch of Endor, identity is disguised to facilitate sin. Knowledge is power, after all, and withholding knowledge about your true identity from someone can give you a degree of power over them.

It is also noteworthy that the true identity of those who disguise themselves in the Bible is always revealed in the end, either intentionally or inadvertently, and the consequences of that follow. 'For there is nothing hidden that will not be disclosed, and nothing concealed that will not be known or brought out into the open' (Luke 8:17).

ACTION, IDENTITY AND CHARACTER

As we have seen from biblical and real-world examples, anonymity may at times facilitate sin. Where there are no apparent consequences in the real world, because an online identity cannot so easily be connected back to us, we can be tempted to act very differently in what we say and do. There have been many cases of trolling (posting inflammatory messages on online forums, with the intention of causing offence and provoking a response) and cyberbullying that have resulted in serious real-world consequences for those involved – many of whom would never have acted that way in real life.

In reality, our online and offline lives are not so easy to compartmentalise. As many people have found out, activity carried out on the web *has* been traced to them. But more fundamentally, the differences between online and offline behaviour raise a critical question here about identity: who are we really?

American basketball player and coach John Wooden is known for his quote, 'The true test of a man's character is what he does when no one is watching.' (Wooden also said, 'Be more concerned with your character than your reputation, because your character is what you really are, while your reputation is merely what others think you are.') By this measure, most of the time in the real world we are judged on our reputation – people's often superficial reaction to our external behaviour – whereas the online world gives greater opportunities for aspects of our true characters to emerge. What we learn about ourselves may surprise us, and may certainly surprise other people.

The mistake that many people make is to assume that how we think and how we act are independent. How we think and feel obviously influences our behaviour: if we feel angry, we are more likely to make an angry response. But what might be less obvious is that our behaviour also affects our thoughts and feelings: how we act influences how we see the world. This is an important principle of Cognitive Behavioural Therapy (CBT). It is a two-way process. Our behaviour can reinforce our assumptions about ourselves and about different situations. It is a little like a book falling open to a favourite page, or a route that becomes so familiar we drive it almost automatically, arriving at our destination with little recollection of the journey itself. Any action can become habitual, including sin, and the temptations online can be far stronger due to the apparent lack of consequences. As English novelist Charles Reade wrote, 'Sow a thought, reap an action; sow an action, reap a habit; sow a habit, reap a character; sow a character, reap a destiny.'

The courses of our lives are seldom determined by a single, exceptional decision. We will all have big decisions to make, and these may have far-reaching impacts: what career we choose, whether we accept a job offer, who we marry, where we live. But who we *are*, the person we *become* – this tends to be a complex patchwork of influences, an interplay between the thousands of everyday situations that arise in our lives, whether large or small, and the way we choose to react to them. These decisions can be self-reinforcing. Author G H Charnley's children's tale tells the story of a skylark who traded his own feathers for worms, until he realised he could no longer fly and was captured by the merchant.[43] Once we set ourselves upon a particular course – whether one we later realise was good or bad – it becomes harder to turn off it. Habits are powerful and the web is a double-edged enabler.

This has keen relevance for our faith. It means that almost everything we do has eternal significance. Every action and decision takes us a step closer to being the person God wants us to be – and that hopefully a part of us wants to be as well – or it takes us a step towards being someone else. As Paul writes in 1 Corinthians 9:24–25, 'Do you not know that in a race all the runners run, but only one gets the prize? Run in such a way as to get the prize. Everyone who competes in the games goes into strict training. They do it to get a crown that will not last; but we do it to get a crown that will last forever.'

Consumerism, our culture's dominant ideology, teaches us that exercising choice is fundamental to our fulfilment. There will be more on this in the next chapter, but choice and change are viewed as the highest good in a consumer society. Ultimately, we are encouraged to define our own identities – to tailor our personal brand that we present to the world to our own individual beliefs, values and interests (even if the way we do that is often through affiliating ourselves with global corporate brands).

---

43 G H Charnley, *The Skylark's Bargain: Thirty-seven talks to boys and girls* (H R Allenson, 1920).

The apparent fluidity of our identities between online and offline worlds naturally impacts our ultimate identity in Christ. Paul writes of Christians who attend church and outwardly practise their faith, but whose so-called private lives fall far short of the standards a truly transformative faith would bring about (1 Corinthians 5 and 6). Amos criticises the Israelites for making an outward show of religion, offering the required sacrifices but not practising justice (Amos 5). This is a recurring theme in the prophets, and it is one we should remember in the context of our supposedly anonymous online lives.

If we truly believed everything we do is seen by the Lord, we would act accordingly, whether online, offline, in public or private. Instead, our online reputation and identity can come ahead of the one we acknowledge to God. 'How can you believe since you accept glory from one another but do not seek the glory that comes from the only God?' (John 5:44).

Connecting with other people is so easy online that we often ignore the principles and safeguards we would insist upon for face-to-face interactions. We take shortcuts, make assumptions, and often don't think too hard about the consequences – simply because it will probably be ok, and the effort or cost of making sure it is safe seems high in comparison to the convenience of otherwise getting the job done in a few clicks.

Additionally, the ease with which people can tailor and edit their own identities on the web extends to our own behaviour. We are necessarily selective in what we disclose online, but the anonymity of the internet can prompt us to stretch the truth. Our identities, who we trust and what we ask others to trust, have practical and spiritual implications.

1. *Be 'wise as serpents, innocent as doves' (Matthew 10:16 ESV).* The anonymity of the web means there is huge scope to allow ourselves to be misled. Don't take the identity of a person or company online for granted, especially if they are asking you to do something (even if it is just clicking on a link). A little extra effort to check that someone is who they say they are can go a long way, whether that's with a web search, looking for reviews and other feedback, or simply holding back a while and seeing how a situation develops to gain more information. Keep the trust you place in someone in proportion with how well you know them.

2. *Get to know people, not profiles.* Recognise that people tailor their personality and behaviour online (this almost certainly includes you, too), even if they don't overtly lie about who they are. The instant-access culture of the web can make us impatient, but it takes time to get to know someone properly. Recognise too that the 'thinner' relationships we have online mean that we can miss vital context – including how people relate with others as well as us – that we might take for granted in real life.

3. *Be WYSIWYG.* There may be a good case for disclosing only very selective details about yourself online; the nature of social networking and the web can mean that you lack control over who has access to the information you post and once you post something online it may never go away. In many instances you may not want to give your real name or other details. However, there is still the question of character and integrity: how do you act online? Do you value and display the same qualities

that you do in other contexts? Does the behaviour of your online profiles reflect the belief that God sees everything?

4. *Invest in understanding your privacy settings.* A few minutes familiarising yourself with these can make a huge difference. Ignoring them can mean anyone has access to personal information that you intended only for friends and family members, or to be shared within a work context. It's a practical point, but like other seemingly simple matters it has spiritual implications.

5. *Don't underestimate the spiritual impacts of good practice.* Making regular backups can be considered a form of insurance that could save you a lot of time, money and frustration, all of which have spiritual implications. Take care when downloading applications and clicking on links – check you really are getting what you're supposed to. Again, this seems like common-sense advice, but it has a spiritual dimension. Perhaps we are more likely not to overlook it if we recognise this.

6. *Entertain an angel.* Who are you when no one else is looking? Remember that actions are habit-forming and character forming, and that your online personality cannot neatly be compartmentalised from the rest of life. Remember too that those with whom you interact online are real people, even if the nature of the web means it's easy to forget that. How we treat people when there are no apparent consequences for us is highly telling about us. As the writer of Hebrews remarks, 'Do not forget to show hospitality to strangers, for by doing so some people have shown hospitality to angels without knowing it' (Hebrews 13:2).

Looking for case studies for this book, there was one I realised I should include but couldn't. Since first getting a smartphone in 2012, I have barely been unplugged for more than a few hours at best. Time, I thought, to draw a line in the sand – not just because I need a useful anecdote but because the more I've worked on the book the less I'm sure who is in charge here.

To begin with, the idea is scary. What if someone wants to get in touch with me and I don't answer? What about the reminders I have set for tasks and meetings? What about the apps I use for online banking, tracking my runs, finding my way to new places? But by the time I get there, I find I am looking forward to a week without it. On the Sunday evening I turn it off, put it on a desk and try to forget about it.

It may be a coincidence, but I sleep better that night. Often I will wake up around 5am and struggle to go back to sleep; years of broken nights with young children and a 24/7 work culture have wrecked my ability to sleep for eight consecutive hours, even when I get the chance.

Strangely, I miss it less than I'm expecting. There are minor inconveniences, of course. I can't read and respond to emails immediately, but apparently the world will keep turning anyway. I have to use the web browser version for online banking, and the interface is terrible. My wife tries to call me about our cat, which needs taking to the vet yet again, cementing his position in the record books as the world's most expensive feline, and gets worried when I don't answer until she remembers I'm not going to have my phone this week. I forget my daughter's medication for the first time in six months, but she still gets it in the end. To give my hands something to do I take up whittling and cut my fingers repeatedly carving a wooden egg.

There are some basic lessons I'll take away from this that I think will make big differences – allowing me to keep the good whilst minimising the harm. (And yes, many of these are no-brainers.) I don't need alerts for every email that comes in; I'll pick them up soon enough anyway. I'll charge my phone in a different room overnight and give myself a clear 9 or 10 hours without it. Maybe only turn it on when I leave the house for work. Make a renewed and concerted effort not to use it at the table. All these things and more add up to create a certain kind of pattern, set of expectations and emotional state: it becomes clear I've been marching to the beat of a drum that isn't playing my tune.[44]

But the thing that concerns me more than any other in my unplugged week is that I have utterly lost all tolerance for boredom. At the beginning, a pause of just seconds, let alone minutes, prompts my thoughts to turn to my phone for relief. This frequently happens at the expense of other interactions. My children, for example, can take what feels like hours to clean their teeth, finish a meal or put on their shoes. These are the times I'm most tempted to check in with the news, social media, and forums for updates on various projects I've been working on. Some of it is meaningful, in isolation, and I need to do it anyway, but ultimately it is distraction from a hiatus in stimulation. I'm reminded of the T S Eliot quote:

Distracted from distraction by distraction
Filled with fancies and empty of meaning
Tumid apathy with no concentration
Men and bits of paper, whirled by the cold wind[45]

And that inability to tolerate boredom, the reflexive reaching for the stream of content to occupy my thoughts, raises a whole other set of issues, which are the subject of the next chapter.

---

44 Yes, it's a mixed metaphor. Sue me.
45 T S Eliot, *The Four Quartets*, 'Burnt Norton', III (Faber & Faber).

5. I CHOOSE, THEREFORE I AM

HOW INFINITE CHOICE IS EXHAUSTING AND UNSATISFYING

By far the most significant insight from being unplugged for a week was the realisation that I use my phone as a distraction from moments of boredom. I know I'm not alone in this quest for distraction. If the figures are correct and we really do check our smartphones every six minutes on average, it's a national epidemic. You only have to look around you – bus stops, people in cafés and restaurants, even in church – to realise that everyone's doing it: nature abhors a vacuum, and so do we. Presented with an awkward couple of minutes without stimulation our default solution is now to pull out the phone.

What are we distracting ourselves from? From my days as a counsellor I know that boredom is rarely about tedium or a lack of interest in a situation. When people say they are bored with something or someone, it's often a form of suppressed anger. Boredom isn't just a lack of engagement, it's a dis-engagement. That suggests we're not distracted by the never-ending stream of content on our devices: we're distracted from the world that is somehow dissatisfying, irritating, frustrating. It's escapism. It's not helped by the fact that boredom is linked to attention failure,[46] which is

---

46 http://www.academia.edu/1912999/The_unengaged_mind_Defining_
boredom_in_terms_of_attention

something that our Always-On culture promotes through the constant temptation to multi-task and consume multiple different streams of content simultaneously. All of this raises a lot more questions, not least because an undertone of anger and cynicism at anything and everything isn't going to do our faith any good – and it means that someone or something else is setting the mood-music for our lives.

The obvious question is what we're bored and angry about. This is where things become a little more speculative and hard to prove, but the circumstantial evidence is strong – bear with me, because this is the crux of the matter.

We are an angry society. We have made an entire industry out of anger. At least one tabloid newspaper seems to specialise in giving angry people a place to earth their anger,[47] a peg to hang it on, blaming one or other group of scapegoats for all the perceived ills we face (migrants, the unemployed, benefits cheats, inept or corrupt politicians, banking fat cats – you get the distinct impression it doesn't matter, so long as there's someone to blame and a target for our righteous indignation). I'm writing this during the American election campaigns. Americans are angry, we're repeatedly told, and Donald Trump is feeding on that to garner support as an anti-establishment candidate. It's not so very different here in the UK, or on the continent. The rise of hate groups, the politics of division, the polarisation of left and right. People are dissatisfied with mainstream politics and they're looking for alternatives. The angrier they are, the more justified they feel in picking a more extreme 'solution'. So here's a working theory as to what's going on.

We've been sold a lie. Repeatedly, pervasively. We've been told we can have whatever we want, whenever we want, and

---

47 Yes, that one. Not named here for legal reasons.

that it will make us happy. It's the myth of consumerism: We have infinite choice, and in that choice lies fulfilment. All we need to do is reach out and access it, taking whatever fits our needs. Consumer goods, brands, online content of all kinds, ideas and even identities – we can shape our worlds around ourselves.

Except it doesn't work. Not just because of the Bible's warnings about seeking happiness in the pursuit of Stuff (Luke 12:15). Consumerism is innately dissatisfying, because that's actually its job. Choice is what it's all about – and there's no point having infinite choice if you don't exercise it. So it has to sow dissatisfaction: the message that happiness is in change, in the next choice – rather than the one you just made, which typically has a rather short half-life. In other words, consumerism promises fulfilment, but it does so by spreading discontent. It's oxymoronic, like the George Carlin quote about fighting for peace. And we distract ourselves from our dissatisfaction with consumerism's predictably failed promise of constant fulfilment by looking for something new to give us a momentary hit of meaning or significance.

If distraction is the chronic cough, then dissatisfaction is the cancer and consumerism is the cigarette smoke. Faith in this kind of environment is challenging at best.

We live in a consumer society. We can buy almost anything we want to, whether goods or services, subject only to whether they are legal and whether we can afford them. (Even affordability isn't necessarily a problem, thanks to the easy availability of credit, and there are often ways around the rules too.) 'People have always made choices but, in the West today, choice has become an ideal which defines our civilisation. Our culture has seen an explosion of choices: we have more sources of entertainment than ever before, we can buy almost whatever we want on the internet, we can go to almost anywhere we want by plane; even our choices of what to eat and drink are wider than ever before.'[48]

The huge array of goods on offer means we have unparalleled choice, and we are encouraged to exercise it. This choice is the crux of the matter: consumerism is about something far more profound than our purchases, or even the content we consume online. 'With so many choices, we imagine ourselves to be individuals and members of our chosen subcultures. Yet our hyper-choice civilisation is bound together by an overarching cultural message which tells us that to choose is to be free. Despite its pluralism contemporary secular culture is unified and dominated by its valorisation of choice.'[49]

The significance of consumerism is the way that the ideal of choice permeates everything we do – what we buy, read and view, as well as how we act, what we believe, and how we present ourselves to the world. The different brands we see advertised everywhere – on TV, billboards, in magazines and on the web – offer not simply a different or better product, but a different and better *lifestyle*. Consumerism encourages us to treat our own lives as a marketing and PR exercise: identifying with the branding and values communicated by different companies as a way to express ourselves, to create our own unique brand and find fulfilment in life.[50]

Consumerism – arguably now our culture's dominant ideology – is therefore not about buying, or consuming. It's not even about choice. It's about what having those choices signifies and enables, and why we're supposed to take them up. In the end, consumerism is about identity: it's the ultimate exercise in self-branding.

Freedom is inherent in the promises consumerism makes to us. It claims to gives us the power to make all the key decisions

---

48 David McIlroy, *Infinite Choice*, Cambridge Papers vol. 22 no. 3, September 2013.
49 David McIlroy, *Infinite Choice*.
50 See further in Guy Brandon, *Free to Live: Expressing the Love of Christ in an Age of Debt* (SPCK, 2010).

in our lives. We are free to be whoever we want, free to express ourselves in the way we see fit and to exercise choices for our own benefit without being restricted by other people. This is the theme of a thousand different advertising campaigns: that we can be whoever we want to be, if we only purchase the right brand of coffee or trainers, use the right deodorant, aspire to the right goods and lifestyle and buy into the right beliefs and values. Even our friendships and relationships are consumerised: there to serve us and maintained only so long as they meet our needs, and discarded for a new one when their usefulness ends. We are encouraged to shape the world around us. With the freedom to mould our own image, our choices bring meaning and self-esteem: as the well-known shampoo advert puts it, '[use this product] because you're worth it'.

Choice is fundamental to consumerism, but so is change, because that is the consequence of exercising choice and the way we maintain our freedom – limiting choices limits our freedom. Thus consumerism teaches us to be dissatisfied and perpetually to strive to keep up with the Joneses. It can't do anything else if it is to encourage us to choose something new.

CONSUMERISM, RELOADED

Consumerism's promise of giving us the power to craft our own identity appeals to us because we lack the anchors that we previously took for granted. Whereas families might once have lived in the same villages or communities for generations, identifying themselves by place and ancestry, we now move around far more for work, study and simply because we can. Professions used to run in families and people were known by the work they did. Marriages were more stable – rates of divorce were low – and people knew not only each other personally, but each others' friends and families too. Some of the most common surnames show the ways we used to 'place' ourselves in the world, by location (Green – living by the village green; Hall, living or working in the Hall of a medieval noble; Wood; Hill), profession (Smith; Taylor; Wright) and family (Wilson, son of William; Johnson, son of John).

The fragmentation of our society and increasing focus on the self, rather than our relationships, means we no longer have these cues. The resulting identity crisis is addressed by filling the void with other ways of understanding who we are. As former Bishop of Maidstone Graham Cray writes:

> *If individualization creates the structure of our society, consumerism provides its dominant ideology and its navigation mechanism or satellite navigation mechanism. Individuals navigate a multichoice world by being consumers.* [51]

This is only the latest phase and the logical conclusion of consumerism, which isn't a particularly recent phenomenon. It probably emerged in something like its present form around the beginning of the twentieth century, but accelerated due to advances in manufacturing and communications technology after the Second World War as it became more cost-effective to create new products and easier than ever before to advertise them. Meanwhile, credit became more widely available (particularly through the introduction and proliferation of credit cards), meaning people had access to money to buy things they would otherwise have had to save for.

The effect of these changes was not just on our spending and borrowing habits, but on our culture. Brands no longer sold goods, they sold lifestyles and identities. Advertising became ever-more sophisticated, segmented to different audiences through different media and subliminal as well as overt. Product placement

---

51 Graham Cray, *Disciples and Citizens: A Vision for Distinctive Living* (IVP, 2007).

encouraged us to associate brands with film and TV characters, implicitly identifying with them when we adopted the same products.

Then, around the turn of the new millennium, the internet brought about a step change in how we engaged with consumer culture. Not only can we now buy almost anything we want to from the comfort of our own homes or from the device in our pockets, thanks to vast and global online stores, but we can seek out whatever information, viewpoints, people and communities we want, because almost any area of interest can be accessed, no matter how unusual. We can tailor our interactions around our own desires, picking and mixing from the endless stream of possibilities on offer.

THE PROS AND CONS OF INFINITE CHOICE

This is, of course, incredibly useful. We have never been more informed as consumers. In fact, 'consumerism' has a second meaning: the consumer movement, which seeks to protect customers by keeping them informed and mandating policies which ensure they are not misled by manufacturers and advertisers. We are empowered. We can choose any product we want on the internet – often on large and well-respected sites like Amazon or eBay – and be fairly sure of prompt delivery, good quality products and protections if we don't receive or don't like what we order. Ratings systems mean we can easily learn which merchants are reliable and honest, and customer feedback means we can find out what products are really like – not just what the advertiser says they are like. Used discerningly, e-commerce is a fantastic development, giving us a greater selection of goods at a better price, and saving us time because we don't need to go out and shop for them at a physical store.

Those benefits can carry through to the rest of our lives. We should have more time to do the things we want and to spend with the people who matter most to us, because we can shop when it's convenient to us and don't have to factor in travel time to a store. We should have extra money thanks to the savings in travel costs and better competition from online stores. Life should be less stressful as we don't have to schedule in a shopping trip in an otherwise busy day – we can wait until the evening or a convenient slot in the day to order what we need.

E-commerce is a prime example of how the web can give us more time, more money, and less stress. As we've seen in previous chapters, those things almost necessarily have an impact on our faith, and the benefits online shopping brings can certainly be used to further our relationship with God and other people. And yet in practice, it doesn't always work out like this.

Consumerism makes a virtue of choice – in fact, exercising choice has become the *greatest* virtue. We are encouraged to do just that, to buy things (and consume content, ideas and values more generally) that we might not otherwise do. How many of us would simply forego a purchase if we couldn't buy it online? It's the classic combination of means, motive and opportunity. We have the money, thanks to credit cards and the availability of debt, as well as historic high levels of disposable income. Advertisers give us a reason to have something new (often spurious, but who's complaining?). And the web makes acquiring it fast and easy. Like any other technology, then, e-commerce is neither good, nor bad, nor neutral in itself: it is a tool in the hands of those who wield it and it implicitly reflects their aims and values. The trick is making sure we use it deliberately and critically – as one of my colleagues discovered when she gave up online shopping for a period of time.

> *I am now over three-quarters of the way into my e-commerce fast. I have given up online shopping (excluding the purchase of tickets for essential travel) for the duration of Lent. Initially my motive was simple*

– to see whether my penchant for shopping online was desensitising me to the dark side of commerce. However, the unintended consequence of this experiment has been the realisation that many of my non-essential purchases were not so much spontaneous as stimulated.

Like millions of people around the world, I was deeply moved by the collapse of the Rana Plaza, a clothing factory in Bangladesh in April 2013.[52] *With an overcrowded and structurally unsound building holding workers on dismal pay and in worse conditions, this really was an accident waiting to happen. Yet why was nothing done? Why were over a thousand lives forfeited? Cheap clothing. Thousands of Bangladeshi people were traumatised, injured or killed at work because the rest of the world wanted cheaper clothes.*

During this experiment the thing that has surprised me most was how aggressive and manipulative the online stores I frequent can be in tempting you back. I'd had barely a fortnight of abstinence before the 'We've missed you – here's 20% off' emails began flooding in. They knew I hadn't been on those sites and it was something of a wake-up call to see the effort invested in just getting me to visit again. They would tap into our human desire to be cared for with phrases like 'You've been quiet' or 'You deserve a treat…' mimicking genuine friendship and demonstrating that pester power isn't always contingent on having kids. Nevertheless, I'm proud to say I've barely browsed. I've come to realise that too often we are prompted into purchases by the offer of a discount or a personalised offer in the post (a £10 off gift voucher arrived from a popular online retailer but with a two-week expiry date, I promptly binned it).

---

52   http://www.bbc.co.uk/news/world-asia-22476774

What has become increasingly apparent is how little we actually need. Even if I am free to shop (and I am free to shop as our offices are directly opposite Cambridge's most popular mall), I tend to wear the same dozen or so outfits to work. Even with a long-standing 'one-in-one-out' policy in my wardrobe and an aversion to hoarding, there are surplus clothes in my wardrobe not to mention unread books on my Kindle and unwatched DVDs on my shelf. In fact, as I cycle almost everywhere, the only thing I actually need to buy each week is food and that's something I've never been particularly extravagant with as cooking for one is rarely much fun.

The result of my online detox has been an offline peace. I have saved so much time by not browsing aimlessly online and surprisingly, not turning an online habit into an offline one. Those hours have been spent on phone calls with loved ones, more mid-week exercise, a more structured prayer life and a regained sense of power over the insidious influence of mass marketing. Still, best of all has been a notable decline in covetousness and discontentment. I consider myself a very content person in general but it was only in deciding not to shop online (which, for me, is essentially not shopping at all) that I realised how much spending time looking at material goods robbed you of that contentment. Drifting through Amazon would remind you of the new Samsung mobile phone which was 'coming soon' or tell you that the box set of the new 'must-see' show was now available. Even if you didn't feel a burning need to buy, just knowing there was new stuff 'out there' feeds the narrative that we are in some way missing out – the social angst of 'FOMO'.[53]

---

53 http://www.forbes.com/sites/work-in-progress/2014/03/27/do-you-have-fomo-fear-of-missing-out/#61cc69142391

Crucially, my experiment has given me a heightened awareness of the various elements which dictate sale patterns including advertising, season and mood. It has also opened my eyes to the complex nature of global supply chains and made me much more conscious of the tacit approval passive purchases can give to unjust systems. I'm certain this new perspective will remain with me far beyond Easter Sunday.[54]

Consumerism is about far more than buying things, and this reality is far more important to recognise than our online shopping habits. We have access to all the information we could possibly want – the useful, the fascinating, the entertaining, the frivolous, the irrelevant, the distracting, and the unpleasant and harmful. There is more available than we can possibly take in. Not only is it difficult to filter the information that we allow through to our computers (censoring the internet is both controversial and practically difficult), but we have trouble filtering out what is important on a personal level, too. 'Analysis paralysis' is the term given to the phenomenon whereby, faced with too much choice, we are unable to make a choice at all. There are so many products, so much information, that we can never consume enough to make a fully informed decision or fully satisfy us. There's always something else.

Additionally, beyond the matters of how we spend our time and money and the headspace we allow or don't allow ourselves, consumerism has serious consequences for our faith. This is because we are taught that the world should suit *my* desires. If we don't like a TV program, we can change to one of dozens or hundreds of other channels to find something else. If we don't like one brand of coffee or toothpaste, we can buy another – there's no shortage of options. If one website doesn't offer the goods or

---

54 Thanks to Njoki Mahiaini, see http://www.jubilee-centre.org/why-i-gave-up-online-shopping/

user experience we want, we find another. (This process typically happens within just seconds: research suggests that it takes a new visitor an average of six to fifteen seconds to decide whether a site is worth staying on. If it loads too slowly, has too many adverts, is complex to navigate or even has too much information – overload is confusing; remember analysis paralysis! – then they will promptly go elsewhere.) If we don't like the boredom of a couple of spare minutes while we're waiting, we can find a distraction online. We tune out or discard what we don't like and replace it with what we do want.

Unfortunately, exactly the same principles can apply to the way we treat our faith. If we don't like a particular verse in the Bible, the way a church conducts its worship or a speaker preaches, or the way we are challenged about particular aspects of our faith, then consumerism teaches us we can leave them behind. That might mean actively deciding we don't believe them, or it might be a more subtle process of tuning them out. Think Jesus' stance on forgiveness is inconvenient? Ignore it and maybe it will go away. Not sure about what the Bible says about sex outside of marriage? Worry about it later, or better still, not at all. Read something challenging about money? Go and find another verse that better represents what you want to hear.

This kind of attitude is exemplified by comments from the secular media (and some Christians), who suggest that the Church should update its teaching to reflect changing social attitudes. That way, goes the argument, it will stop being so offensive and may not be written off as irrelevant. The implication and the irony are that our highly fluid social mores should provide the standard by which the unchanging Creator and his Word are deemed valid, rather than vice versa. Our faith is tailored around what *we* want, not viewed as a source of authority that shapes our lives and characters, or has anything meaningful, authoritative or transformational to say to society.

ME-CENTRED MORALITY

Where consumerism really comes unstuck from Christian teaching is its understanding of freedom. It is an attractive idea and, like the best lies, it's close to the truth. As theologian David McIlroy writes, 'The message that choice equals freedom contains some truth: I enjoy greater freedom than a prisoner because my choices about what to do with my time are subject to fewer constraints. My ability to play a part, through voting, in choosing my country's government, gives me a measure of political freedom which the citizens of Syria do not currently enjoy.'[55] It intuitively seems right: choice equals freedom is a simple enough equation. But there is a serious distortion about the nature of freedom inherent in our adoption of consumerism as a guiding ideology.

At the deepest level, consumerism tells me that I have the power to shape the world around myself, making my own choices about everything that affects me, whether that is what I wear and the music I listen to, or the values to which I aspire and the lifestyle choices I exercise. I make myself in my own image. The allusion to Genesis 1:26 should be obvious: 'Then God said, "Let us make mankind in our image, in our likeness, so that they may rule over the fish in the sea and the birds in the sky, over the livestock and all the wild animals, and over all the creatures that move along the ground."'

The implications of setting ourselves up as the centre of our worlds should also be clear. Consumerism is, at heart, just another form of idolatry: the worship of the self instead of God.

No wonder, then, that it comes with an erosion of the moral authority of Scripture, as we downgrade the Bible's teachings to just another set of lifestyle choices, to be adopted only if they are interesting, useful and convenient to us. We lose the ability to speak out: in an environment of infinite choice, any choice is valid.

---

55 David McIlroy, *Infinite Choice*, Cambridge Papers vol. 22 no. 3, September 2013.

Choice is intrinsically personal, so criticising someone's lifestyle choices is tantamount to criticising their very identity.

Author Dale Kuehne calls our environment of postmodern individualistic consumerism the 'iWorld' (which has a better ring to it), after tech giant Apple's series of devices. Steve Jobs' 'i' prefix brilliantly illustrates the essence of the age in which we live: iPod, iPad, iPhone, iWorld. Writing about the changing sexual standards that comprises one of consumerism's key freedoms but with an eye to wider culture, he argues that there are only three restrictions to freedom in the iWorld:

1. One may not criticise someone else's life choices or behaviour.
2. One may not behave in a manner that coerces or causes harm to others.
3. One may not engage in a sexual relationship with someone without his or her consent.[56]

Whilst we would agree with at least the third point without question, the real implication of these rules taken together is that so long as it doesn't harm anyone else, I can do whatever I want. I allow people the freedom to act as they wish without judging them, and I expect to be treated the same way. This applies in any and every sphere of life: sex, relationships, shopping, religion, whatever personal decision or lifestyle choice I take.

What we don't tend to realise is that our definition of 'harm' is almost as me-centred as everything else we do. Consumerism places so much emphasis on personal choice and what is right for us that other concerns fade to secondary importance at best. The effects of a consensual sexual affair on a spouse or children; the routine use of conflict minerals in the supply of materials for consumer electronics; the child labour and human rights abuses that are a common part of the clothing industry; the effects of

---

56 Dale Kuehne, *Sex and the iWorld: Rethinking Relationship Beyond an Age of Individualism* (Baker Academic, 2009), p. 71.

climate change and impact on some of the most vulnerable people on the planet that result from our collective addiction to fossil fuels; the unsustainable use of natural resources to create the products we buy; the long-term effects on us and our families of a decision to take on an unnecessary debt. These are just some of the examples of the factors consumerism downplays, because it is my right to exercise choice and that tends to trump consequences that we cannot directly see, or that are deemed acceptable because everyone else is doing them or because changing them is too difficult and would entail too great a sacrifice. There is something inherently self-justifying about consumerism – as if, imperfect though my choices might be rendered by their unpalatable if invisible consequences, taking away my choices would be a far, far worse evil.

Viewed in this light, consumerism's 'valorisation of choice' appears in a different light. For starters, my choices are often taken at the expense of someone else's freedom. My empowerment comes at the cost of someone else's disempowerment. Additionally, if I want to stay free, I am forced to keep choosing: paradoxically, my freedom is contingent upon remaining subject to the tyranny of constant choice. Oops.

Thus the 'freedom' that consumerism offers us is very different to the freedom we have in Christ. Consumerism is the enemy of love, commitment and faithfulness that God holds out towards us and that we should be mirroring in our own lives. Its demands on us to buy and consume more, continually to change and exercise new choices, have diverse and far-reaching impacts on us, other people and the natural world.

Being connected is empowering. We can access goods, services and information to a degree that was unimaginable twenty years ago. We have more choice than ever before – something that brings potentially huge rewards in terms of allowing us to save money, save time, and reduce stress. However, our culture's belief in the all-consuming importance of that choice has serious implications for our faith, since we are encouraged to shape our world in our own image.

1. *Be a critical consumer.* Christians are supposed to be fish out of water, 'aliens and strangers' in the world. Mainstream consumer culture should appear foreign to us if we have taken on board the truth of the gospel. Recognise that there is an agenda behind the ideas and values we are routinely 'sold' through advertising, news media and entertainment, and that these will rarely coincide with those of our faith.

2. *Think before you spend.* PayPal and one-click ordering make it so straightforward to buy something we see and like online that it can become an almost unconscious process. Consumerism goes far beyond e-commerce, but the ease with which we can buy almost anything we want reinforces the assumption that it is my right to have what I want and push the potential consequences to the back of our minds. Pausing before we click and proceed to checkout is also a helpful brake on the way that advertising seeks to influence us – reminding us who is in charge of our wallets as well as our loyalty and values.

3. *Be an informed customer.* When you do buy, use the information available to you to make really good purchases – whether this means ones that are high quality and durable (reducing unnecessary waste), created from sustainable resources, or with transparency and justice throughout the supply chain. Your money constitutes a vote for the company from which you are buying and the practices and values they endorse. How can you honour kingdom values in this purchase?

4. *Pick your battles.* It is one thing to keep ourselves informed, quite another to be perfectly informed. Having access to infinite choice can be exhausting, and it can prevent us from making a decision as we seek to keep our options open, wary of making the wrong choice. In this respect, the best can be the enemy of the good. There will usually come a point when the information you have gathered is good enough and you should make a choice. This is equally true of elements of your faith as it is of an online purchase. You could 'shop' for the right church indefinitely, never committing to settling in one place and becoming a part of the community, because you are concerned you might be missing out on a better church elsewhere.

5. *Track your finances.* Credit cards and online payments mean that it's very easy to pay for shopping on the web, and easy to go into debt. In the worst instances, debt constitutes a form of slavery, locking us into a cycle of never-ending payments through high interest rates. It reduces our freedom and prevents us from living out our faith to the degree we might. For example, we may not be able to give as generously because that money is going to a credit card company. We might be forced to work more hours to pay our debts, perhaps at the weekend

or other antisocial times, preventing us from spending that time with family and friends. Debt is also linked to stress, anxiety and depression.

6. *Challenge yourself with new viewpoints.* The consumer landscape is one that perfectly fits the individual: you can shape your world around your own needs and desires. This means we can surround ourselves with people and opinions that match our own, never really challenging ourselves to think differently or look outside our own comfortable bubble. This might involve finding out about political or religious views that differ from your own, or learning new things about other subjects (food, health, entertainment, etc.) that you might not have done before. There is of course a risk here too: as well as being an environment in which we can confine ourselves to a self-selected bubble of viewpoints, the consumer world can be one in which we try anything and everything.

7. *Use the benefits of online shopping wisely.* E-commerce can and should in theory result in us having more money, more time and less stress. We can either use these benefits well or squander them. When you save money and time, be deliberate about how you then spend these God-given resources.

8. *Take a break from online shopping.* If online shopping has an unhelpful hold on you, perhaps because it has become an unthinking habit, then commit to taking a break for a week or a month. It may be that you continue to purchase essentials over the web (like a weekly food shop) but decide to stop spending discretionary income online for a while, in order to ensure your purchases are more deliberate and thought-through. Aim to use

the time you would have browsed e-commerce sites in other activities, including prayer and Bible study, and furthering other relationships.

Consumerism is inherently me-centred: it tells me I can and should shape the world around myself, with secondary regard – at best – for other people. Communications technology, ironically (since it facilitates relationship with others), reinforces this idea and gives us abundant choice, thereby allowing us to choose from a greater variety of things that suit us.

Despite this focus on the self, technology is a corporate matter; its effects range from the personal right through to the global. As an example of a technological innovation that had unforeseen consequences at almost every level of society, consider the invention of the cotton gin:

> *Eli Whitney's cotton gin revolutionised the textiles trade in America in the nineteenth century. Previously, separating cotton fibres from the seeds was a time-consuming and labour intensive task. Whitney's design suddenly made cotton hugely profitable, creating many fortunes and reshaping the American South as a global economic power – giving rise to major new shipping ports, the development of new machinery and technical innovation which arguably paved the way for the Industrial Revolution.*
>
> *It also vastly increased the demand for slave labour, to grow and pick cotton for the new machinery and the thriving international trade in cotton. By 1860 around a third of the population of the southern states were slaves. The cotton gin was therefore also an indirect cause of the American Civil War, in which 620,000 Union and Confederate soldiers were killed between 1861 and 1865 – more than any other American war in history.*

If this was true of the cotton gin, it is also true of the internet. There is no area of life that has not been impacted by the

*information revolution. And yet, the me-centredness of
our approach means we don't always recognise that. The
flow of data is two-way, which means that when we access
information from 'the web' – a misleadingly vague term
that ignores the individual users, ISPs, hosting companies,
governments and other bodies that are involved in different
forms along the way – there is plenty of scope for 'the web'
to access information from us, too. And this, more than we
might at first realise, has implications for our freedom and
our faith.*

6. BIG BROTHER

WHY IT MATTERS THAT YOU'RE BEING WATCHED

'We were shocked and outraged by the deadly act of terrorism in San Bernardino last December. We mourn the loss of life and want justice for all those whose lives were affected. The FBI asked us for help in the days following the attack, and we have worked hard to support the government's efforts to solve this horrible crime. We have no sympathy for terrorists.

When the FBI has requested data that's in our possession, we have provided it. Apple complies with valid subpoenas and search warrants, as we have in the San Bernardino case. We have also made Apple engineers available to advise the FBI, and we've offered our best ideas on a number of investigative options at their disposal.

We have great respect for the professionals at the FBI, and we believe their intentions are good. Up to this point, we have done everything that is both within our power and within the law to help them. But now the US government has asked us for something we simply do not have, and something we consider too dangerous to create. They have asked us to build a backdoor to the iPhone.

Specifically, the FBI wants us to make a new version of the iPhone operating system, circumventing several important security features, and install it on an iPhone recovered during the investigation. In the wrong hands, this software — which does not exist today — would have the potential to unlock any iPhone in someone's physical possession.

The FBI may use different words to describe this tool, but make no mistake: Building a version of iOS that bypasses security in this way would undeniably create a backdoor. And while the government may argue that its use would be limited to this case, there is no way to guarantee such control.'

Statement by Apple CEO Tim Cook[57]

The 'FBiOS' case that came to a head in February 2016 perfectly highlights some of the tensions inherent in the freedoms that communications technologies bring.[58] The same technology that allows us to communicate so easily with other people can be used to spy on us; the same technologies that allow us to keep data secure from hackers and criminals can also be used to hide evidence of serious crime.

The Internet is the most liberating tool for humanity ever invented, and also the best for surveillance. It's not one or the other. It's both.

JOHN PERRY BARLOW, CYBER-RIGHTS ACTIVIST

It is now clear that surveillance of all kinds – by governments, domestic and foreign; by corporations; by criminal organisations and individuals – is taking place on an unprecedented and indiscriminate scale. Some people see this as an infringement of our liberties and a gross invasion of our privacy. Others accept it as

---

57 http://www.apple.com/customer-letter/
58 On this occasion, the FBI ultimately found a way to circumvent the iPhone's security without direct help from Apple. https://www.washingtonpost.com/world/national-security/fbi-paid-professional-hackers-one-time-fee-to-crack-san-bernardino-iphone/2016/04/12/5397814a-00de-11e6-9d36-33d198ea26c5_story.html

a necessary concession in the fight against terrorism and a property of the world in which we live. Although this is a fast-moving area, questions around surveillance and the harvesting of personal data are not going away in a hurry. The Bible's principles are timeless, if not its cultural settings. Is this mass surveillance and erosion of privacy something Christians should be concerned about – and if so, what can we do about it?

YOU ARE BEING WATCHED

Barely a week goes by without fresh revelations of covert surveillance of one kind or another, or of a company that has lost customer information to a hacker. Our personal details and other data are routinely collected or acquired by a large number and range of organisations and individuals – and the line between them isn't always as clear as you might think.

Revelations from whistle-blowing website WikiLeaks[59] over the past few years have made public the degree of mass surveillance routinely practised by governments, as well as the amount of information shared between them. Documents leaked by defence contractor Edward Snowden in 2013 showed that the National Security Agency (NSA) was collecting huge amounts of information from US citizens, including phone records, text messages and internet browsing habits. The NSA was able to gain access to Google's and Yahoo's data centres. Working with the NSA, the UK's Government Communication Headquarters (GCHQ) has collected and shared data tapped from fibre-optic cables around the world. Snowden's documents showed that GCHQ has been accessing enormous quantities of personal information – emails, Facebook posts, internet histories and phone calls – and sharing it

---

59 See wikileaks.org, but bear in mind that searching for, visiting and especially supporting the site will likely get you flagged for further attention by the NSA and GCHQ. https://wikileaks.org/nsa-gchq-spying

with the NSA, all of which was 'being carried out without any form of public acknowledgement or debate'.[60]

One of the major justifications for this level of surveillance is that it enables the authorities to protect us from terrorist attacks and organised crime. Whilst this problem is not something to be taken lightly, criminals are also capable of protecting their communications, of encrypting email and using various tools to browse the web anonymously. (Islamic State routinely uses encrypted messaging to communicate securely, for example.) Equally, mass surveillance is not the only way to catch them. There is a thriving debate about how effective mass surveillance is in helping the authorities to pinpoint terrorists, or predict attacks, or whether it even poses a distraction from more specific intelligence about a threat.[61] A number of attacks, such as the Charlie Hebdo murders in France in January 2015, the Paris attacks of 13 November 2015, and the Boston Marathon bombing of 15 April 2013, have been carried out despite the perpetrators already being known to the authorities or on watchlists; the problem was often not that the authorities did not have enough information, but that they did not have the resources to follow up on the leads they already *did* have. 'Mass data collectors can dig deeply into anyone's digital persona but don't have the resources to do so with everyone. Surveillance of the entire population, the vast majority of whom are innocent, leads to the diversion of limited intelligence resources in pursuit of huge numbers of false leads. Terrorists are comparatively rare, so finding one is a needle-in-a-haystack problem. You don't make it easier by throwing more needleless hay on the stack.'[62]

---

60 http://www.theguardian.com/uk/2013/jun/21/gchq-cables-secret-world-communications-nsa

61 http://arstechnica.co.uk/tech-policy/2015/11/terrorist-attacks-mass-surveillance-is-the-problem-not-the-solution/

62 http://www.slate.com/articles/health_and_science/new_scientist/2015/01/mass_surveillance_against_terrorism_gathering_intelligence_on_all_is_statistically.html

The state is not the only party that collects our personal information on a vast scale. Mass harvesting of data by companies has also become the norm. Search engines and social networks collect information to help them match adverts to users' personal interests. This is a core part of their business model, since most of these sites are free to users. However, the practices often extend to monitoring users' complete browsing habits, including the sites they visit, what they click on, what they buy – with or without the customers' consent,[63] and sometimes even whether they are actually logged in or not.

As well as those instances where a company deliberately harvests information to learn more about us themselves, there are instances in which the technology they offer us is open to abuse. In 2006 search engine AOL accidentally released a database of 21 million search queries from 650,000 users, representing a period of three months.[64] The database was copied before it could be taken down, and is still searchable online today (a cautionary tale that what goes online can stick around forever). Even though no names were released, each record is tagged with a user number and can be cross-referenced with other search queries – making it straightforward to build up a profile of those involved.

More recently, in February 2015 Samsung – the world's largest technology company – warned customers not to discuss any personal details in front of the voice-activated TV sets. 'If your spoken words include personal or other sensitive information, that information will be among the data captured and transmitted to a third party.'[65] (This immediately prompted comparisons with George Orwell's famous novel *1984*, in which state authorities spy on citizens through two-way monitors called telescreens.) At the end of 2015, electronic toymaker VTech was hacked and

---

63 One of the problems is that people simply don't read the Terms and Conditions (which are often extensive and boring) before clicking to confirm their agreement.
64 http://news.cnet.com/2100-1030_3-6103098.html
65 http://www.bbc.co.uk/news/technology-31296188

details about more than six million people were stolen – names, email addresses, encrypted passwords, IP addresses and other data including children's names, dates of birth and gender, and even pictures of them. The company had omitted to take basic precautions,[66] such as communicating passwords and sensitive information over encrypted connections.[67] And, of course, there is the infamous Ashley Madison 'affairs dating' website hack, in which 25 gigabytes of data – including user names, real names, credit card details and other personal information for users, as well as a large number of internal documents and corporate emails – was hacked and released on the web.[68]

Neither is it just big businesses. Smaller companies are often targeted because they are typically less security conscious, and lack the budgets and expertise to protect data as robustly as large corporations can (at least, in theory). Churches fall into this category, and typically possess a large amount of sensitive information: names, addresses, emails, phone numbers, bank account details, and further information for employees and volunteers. Yet comparatively few churches use all the tools they could to prevent a breach: encryption, regular software updates and malware checks, firewalls, and so on. Computers may be shared between employees and volunteers and proper security practices may be overlooked.

The details that cyber criminals steal are frequently sold on to other criminals who can make use of them, whether to maintain spam email lists or to steal money and make illegal purchases. Executives of major companies are often the target of cyberattacks when travelling, but any of us may be susceptible to computer viruses, worms and other forms of malware that seek to steal or destroy data, or to use our computers to carry out illegal activities.[69]

66 http://www.bbc.co.uk/news/technology-35027504
67 http://www.bbc.co.uk/news/technology-34971337
68 http://arstechnica.com/security/2015/08/ashley-madison-hack-is-not-only-real-its-worse-than-we-thought/
69 http://www.bbc.co.uk/news/technology-30001424

Illegal botnets ('robot networks' of computers that have been taken control of, usually without their owners' knowledge) are used to send spam emails, attack websites, steal personal data and recruit other computers to the botnet. They can consist of millions or even tens of millions of computers.

Even for legitimate collection of information (whatever that may mean), our privacy relies on the strength of other organisations' practices, not just our own. Data is not always stored securely, meaning that theft by hackers from governments and businesses is commonplace – the publication of celebrities' photos from Apple's iCloud storage in 2014 being one of many examples.[70] Governments frequently request and receive data from web companies in the course of legal investigations. In the first six months of 2014, almost 35,000 government requests for users' data were made (globally) to Facebook alone. Requests for user information from Google have risen 150 per cent in the last five years.[71] The public sector frequently contracts out work to the private sector, raising issues around confidentiality of information such as medical records, amongst other things.

Then there are the rogue governments that exploit security loopholes to gather information or carry out cyber warfare. One of the most high-profile examples of this was North Korea's hack of Sony pictures, in response to their proposed release of *The Interview* – a satirical film about two journalists tasked with assassinating the country's leader, Kim Jong Un. A huge amount of sensitive information was stolen and leaked online, including personal emails, information about employees and their families, personal photos, salary details and even unreleased films. Closer to home, evidence suggests that the NSA has had a long-term programme of infiltrating computers and placing highly sophisticated malware on them – hidden software designed to monitor users and disrupt

---

70 In this case, targeted attempts were made via 'phishing' to learn individuals' iCloud usernames and passwords.
71 http://www.bbc.co.uk/news/business-29910101

certain activities.[72] GCHQ also carries out CNE – computer network exploitation – at home and overseas. This includes the ability to activate cameras and microphones on mobile devices remotely.[73] In some countries, mass surveillance of the web is undeniably used as a tool to control the population.

Understanding the threat posed by free access to information, China's authorities have implemented a broad range of measures to control internet use – known collectively by critics as 'The Great Firewall of China'. The government routinely monitors individual users and blocks website content with the intention of preventing citizens from accessing information that could harm national unity, incite people to overthrow the government, spread mistruths or destroy the order of society, promote unwanted material and services (from gambling and sexual content to proscribed religions and movements, such as Falun Gong).

The background to the Great Firewall of China is former leader Deng Xiaoping's belief that 'If you open the window for fresh air, you have to expect some flies to blow in.' The freedom of cultural and market reforms also opened the window to ideologies that did not fit with the values of China's ruling classes. Measures to control internet access include IP blocking, DNS and URL filtering, packet filtering and man-in-the-middle attacks, amongst others. These either prevent individuals from accessing sites, or monitor their communications.

In practice, tech-savvy Chinese web users have found ways to circumvent ('climb') the Wall using Tor or VPNs (virtual private networks), enabling people to avoid censorship and protest against the government. However, the penalties if caught can be harsh:

'*A frequent topic of conversation among my friends here has been: Who will be arrested next?*

---

72 http://arstechnica.com/security/2015/02/how-omnipotent-hackers-tied-to-the-nsa-hid-for-14-years-and-were-found-at-last/

73 http://www.independent.co.uk/news/uk/politics/gchq-hacking-phones-and-computers-is-legal-says-top-uk-court-a6871716.html

Some of us met recently for dinner and started a list of potential candidates. We included outspoken scholars, writers and lawyers who have discussed democracy and freedom, criticized the government and spoken out for the disadvantaged.

Some of my dinner companions nominated themselves for the list. We agreed that the social critic Xiao Shu (the pen name of Chen Min) and Guo Yushan, a friend of the blind lawyer Chen Guangcheng (now in the United States), should top the list. I'm right behind them.

Almost all of us are active microbloggers. Some of us qualify as Big V, the widely used label for influential bloggers with millions of followers. (V stands for "verified account".) It is our online activism that makes us prime targets of the government.

In August, the authorities launched the most severe round yet in their "campaign against cybercrime". Ostensibly to curtail online "rumors," they are rounding up and jailing outspoken netizens across the country. Judging from official media accounts and police reports, the number of arrests is in the hundreds, and many of us believe it may be in the thousands.

Charles Xue, a government critic and a Big V blogger with 12 million followers, who writes under the name Xue Manzi, was arrested as an early high-profile example. He was detained in August for allegedly hiring prostitutes, but the state-run news agency, Xinhua, made clear the true reason: "This has sounded a warning bell about the law to all Big V's on the Internet." The most infamous case was the arrest of a 16-year-old boy in Gansu Province. In early September, he posted two short messages commenting on the police's handling of a mysterious death. His message included the phrase:

*"All officials shield one another." He was arrested a few
days later.*

*Meanwhile, the state media have published a steady
flow of articles warning microbloggers to tone down their
commentaries. An Aug. 24 editorial on Xinhua's web
site said that popular bloggers who "poison the online
environment" should be "dealt with like rats scurrying
across the street that everyone wants to kill."* [74]

WHAT DOES THE BIBLE SAY ABOUT MASS SURVEILLANCE?

It goes without saying that the specific issues raised by modern
communications technology and our highly-connected lifestyles
were not and could not have been a feature of life in biblical times.
Nevertheless, the Bible has plenty to say about the questions posed
by mass surveillance – both from the perspective of the watchers,
and the watched.

When discussing something so alien to the kind of society
described in the Bible, there is always a temptation to take the
easy way out and offer a superficial analysis based on a handful
of proof texts. On the surface of it, there are many verses in the
Bible that appear to speak to our concerns around surveillance.
One of the most common counter-arguments from Christians is:
'If you're not doing anything wrong, you have nothing to worry
about' (something that will strike a chord with the victims of
the Ashley Madison hack). The Bible is full of warnings against
hidden misdeeds and encouragements to integrity: 'For there
is nothing hidden that will not be disclosed, and nothing
concealed that will not be known and brought out into the
open' (Luke 8:17). And, unlike even the most intrusive surveillance

---

74 http://www.nytimes.com/2013/10/16/opinion/murong-busting-chinas-
bloggers.html?_r=0

practices, God sees absolutely *everything*. 'You have searched me, Lord, and you know me. You know when I sit and when I rise; you perceive my thoughts from afar. You discern my going out and my lying down; you are familiar with all my ways. Before a word is on my tongue you, Lord, know it completely' (Psalm 139:1–4).

Such verses may be a helpful reminder to act in such a way *as if* our actions were publicly known, but it falls far short in offering a thoughtful and balanced response to the problems raised by mass surveillance and the loss of privacy that this entails.

Although until relatively recently there was no internet, no phones or cameras, surveillance itself is nothing new and neither are ways of circumventing it. The biblical writers themselves occasionally used simple codes to identify people and places. Informed readers would know what they were talking about, but the authors would not risk the anger of the authorities. In the book of Revelation, John references the emperor Nero with a code. 'This calls for wisdom. Let the person who has insight, let him calculate the number of the beast, for it is the number of a man. His number is 666.'[75] (Revelation 13:18) Due to the risks of being arrested by watchful and hostile authorities, early Christians also used codes and symbols to identify themselves to one another without others knowing, including the fish.

We may take both religious freedoms and our use of communications technology for granted. In other countries, hostile authorities routinely track Christians using mobile phone signals and internet activity, as well as more conventional methods, and they may face imprisonment, torture or death if they are caught. 'Christian converts in Iran – and any Christians who minister among individuals from a Muslim background –

---

75 The Greek word means to 'calculate by gematria', a system used by the Jews that involved substituting numbers for letters. 666 is a number that corresponds to the Aramaic words *Neron Caesar*, or Nero, the emperor who lived from AD 37 to 68 and was responsible for burning and crucifying hundreds of Christians.

know they are either already being monitored by the Ministry of Intelligence and Security (MOIS), or that MOIS may identify them and begin monitoring at any time. "If you talk to anyone, they are very careful about phones. They know they can't send emails or Skype ... they have to be very careful about where they meet, how they meet ... everyone says the same story. The constant theme is pressure.""[76]

Nevertheless, even for the West, mass surveillance and the loss of our privacy have serious implications for us and for our faith.

WHY SHOULD WE CARE?

Any state or corporation that is capable of mass surveillance is, by definition, extremely powerful. The will and ability to monitor such a large number of people in such detail represents a huge concentration of political, financial and technological power. The concentration of power, and the abuses that tend to arise from it, is one of the issues that the Bible points to with regards to surveillance. As we saw in previous chapters, the Israelites found themselves subject to such abusive and unaccountable power many times in their history, first in Egypt and then at the hands of the Assyrians, Babylonians and Romans, amongst others.

What all forms of mass surveillance have in common is that the information collected with them can be used to control people – if that is not its explicit purpose in the first place. Knowledge truly is power and the more you know about someone, the better you can predict their behaviour and the more you can influence it. This is one of the major premises of the 2015 Bond film *Spectre* (spoiler alert).

---

76 See for example http://www.christiansinparliament.org.uk/uploads/ APPGs-report-on-Persecution-of-Christians-in-Iran.pdf

Viewing existing methods as unnecessary and obsolete in the twenty-first century, Max Denbigh ('C'), the head of the new Joint Intelligence Service, plans to decommission the 'double-o' programme in favour of a system of mass surveillance and data sharing across several countries: the Nine Eyes programme. The new initiative is about to go online, giving the security services unprecedented access to intelligence streams from all around the world.

Meanwhile Bond investigates a shadowy organisation run by Franz Oberhauser – a man thought to have died in an avalanche twenty years earlier, and who has since taken on a new identity as Ernst Stavro Blofeld. Blofeld's organisation, which profits from drugs and human trafficking, terrorism and arms sales, has funded the Nine Eyes programme due to the strategic importance of surveillance for its activities.

Spectre, whilst fictional, raises the issue that any information collected – even for the right purposes – may be accessed or used by those with less benign motives, whether that happens to mean terrorists, cyber thieves, disgruntled employees or misguided civil servants. In ancient Israel, the centralisation of the monarchy (which was not God's original plan for the nation) led to vulnerabilities and injustice. Some of Israel's own kings were evil, such as Manasseh; in other instances, a weak king was incited to evil by another party, as the case of Ahab and Jezebel. In each case, the centralisation of power meant there was a 'single point of failure' that could be exploited.

Power enables its holders to control others, and the temptation is always to do so even if the reasons power was initially assumed are honourable. In the case of the state, there may be a presumption of guilt: everyone is a suspect and requires monitoring. This turns on its head the principle of 'innocent until proven guilty' that is included in many legal codes and constitutions – hardly ensuring we are treated as blameless parties until it is established otherwise.[77] Corporations use the data they gather to influence our behaviour for financial gain. For cyber criminals, the control is more overt.

Whilst mass surveillance, and the concentration of political and/or financial power it entails, has implications for all of us, it raises particularly serious questions for Christians.

Firstly, we collude with this surveillance and the culture that goes along with it. Any organisation capable of carrying out such activities is, by its very nature, extremely powerful. The problem with the powerful and centralised state is that it tends to be distant and neglectful at best, abusive at worst (as the Israelites found out in Egypt, and countless other people have experienced since). Large corporations, too, are able to take the law into their own hands and act as they wish; concentrated power, whether financial or political, risks becoming unaccountable for its actions and does not serve its constituents' interests. By turning a blind eye to the issues posed by mass surveillance, we are tacitly endorsing the powers that lie behind it, along with the abuses that can and often do result.

Secondly, as we argued in earlier chapters, when we allow another party this much power, we are giving away control over our lives – allowing ourselves to be manipulated and potentially enslaved.

Surveillance does not just raise philosophical issues about whether it is acceptable or harmful to watch over people's

---

77 Early in 2014, for example, hundreds of academics from around the world signed a declaration of their opposition to mass surveillance, part of which read, 'Without privacy people cannot freely express their opinions or seek and receive information. Moreover, mass surveillance turns the presumption of innocence into a presumption of guilt. Nobody denies the importance of protecting national security, public safety, or the detection of crime. But current secret and unfettered surveillance practices violate fundamental rights and the rule of law, and undermine democracy.' http://www.academicsagainstsurveillance.org/

shoulders. The information collected is put to use, whether by the original gatherer or by someone who later acquires it, and those uses may be far from benign. A recent BBC documentary explored how the vast amount of data collected can be used to predict our behaviour and, by extension, be used as a form of control. Rather than just looking at the content of our communications, 'traffic analysis' or looking at patterns of communication is particularly fruitful in predicting individuals' actions in the future. 'The power of that data to predict and analyse what we're going to do is very, very high. And giving that power to somebody else, regardless of the original or stated intentions, is very worrying.'[78]

What happens if those who gather information change their policies and use their powers to carry out harmful activities? Or if they work with authorities who have different values? Or if the jurisdiction in which the data was collected does not respect the privacy rights of non-nationals (as is the case in the US)? In 2004 Shi Tao, a Chinese journalist, was arrested and imprisoned for ten years on state secrets charges after leaking details to a human rights group from a secret memorandum warning of activities by democracy activists, amongst other things. The evidence against him included material about his personal email account provided by web company Yahoo![79] The US led the way in calling for the laws to be changed after this event, but the picture has changed over the last decade, especially after Edward Snowden's revelations about the extent of government surveillance. Today, web companies are more likely to be suing the government for breaching the right to free speech through their surveillance practices (as in the case of Twitter and the US government).[80]

In other countries, mass surveillance is a tool of state repression; after the ongoing protests sparked by the Arab Spring, Egyptian

78 Dr Joss Wright, Oxford Internet Institute. http://www.bbc.co.uk/news/technology-29032399

79 http://www.hrw.org/node/11259/section/12

80 http://www.abc.net.au/news/2014-10-08/twitter-suing-us-government-for-breaching-freedom-of-speech/5799666

authorities called for tenders to carry out indiscriminate mass surveillance of social media in the country.[81]

On a less dramatic but still concerning scale, the knowledge gained by web companies can be used to influence our behaviour. This may be carried out in the interests of providing a more targeted and effective service for us, and may be as routine as showing us particular adverts to try to get us to buy products that match our interests. However, the line between these practices and outright manipulation – even exploitation – is a fine one. There is growing evidence of companies offering different prices for goods and services based on your online profile and browsing history. This has particularly been observed in the case of airlines, which change their prices based on a wide variety of factors already.[82] Use a different browser or different computer, and you could be charged more or less.

The amount of information means that many large companies know a huge amount about us – including, thanks to GPS technology embedded in our smartphones, where we are at any given time.[83] This can easily be abused by corporations, or individuals within those corporations who have access to the data. Cyberstalking is a frequent component of domestic abuse and a large range of apps exist to track other people and monitor their actions (right down to logging every keystroke and pinpointing their precise location).

BOILING FROGS

If you drop a frog in a pot of boiling water, it will of course frantically try to clamber out. But if you place it

81 http://www.amnesty.org/en/news/egypt-s-attack-internet-privacy-tightens-noose-freedom-expression-2014-06-04

82 http://www.usatoday.com/story/travel/columnist/mcgee/2013/04/03/do-travel-deals-change-based-on-your-browsing-history/2021993/

83 http://theweek.com/articles/441995/uber-growing-threat-corporate-surveillance

gently in a pot of tepid water and turn the heat on low,
it will float there quite placidly. As the water gradually
heats up, the frog will sink into a tranquil stupor,
exactly like one of us in a hot bath, and before long,
with a smile on its face, it will unresistingly allow itself
to be boiled to death.[84]

'Boiling frog syndrome' has become a metaphor for the idea that people will accept gradual change relatively unthinkingly, even if the end result is something that they would strenuously resist if it was made all at once.[85] The kind of disempowerment we face is subtle and incremental. It is a gradual erosion of liberties, little by little, until we realise that we are very far from where we started and have no easy way to get back there.

Imagine if, twenty years ago when the internet started taking hold, you had been told it would one day be possible for strangers to view photos of your family, discover your private email, phone number and physical address, and for companies to track every site you visited, to know your shopping habits and pinpoint your whereabouts in real-time – and that you yourself would be providing most of the information that made this possible. It is almost unthinkable we would have agreed to it. But that is the situation in which we now find ourselves. Today, 90 per cent of people accept that we have lost control of our personal data.[86]

How did this happen? Incrementally, of course. You sign up for your first email address, a profile on a social network. Perhaps you're not too careful about privacy settings. You sign up for other

---

84   Daniel Quinn, *The Story of B* (Bantam, 1996), p. 258.
85   Experiments in the nineteenth century suggested that the principle was correct, although a low rate of change of temperature is critical to gain the frog's tacit agreement in the enterprise; more recently, experts in amphibian temperature regulation have found that frogs are more interested in self-preservation than earlier scientists gave them credit for. True or not, it remains a useful analogy.
86   http://www.pcworld.com/article/2846855/control-over-personal-info-nearly-dead-pew-survey-respondents-say.html

apps and services using the same email and social network profile, agreeing to the Terms and Conditions without reading them, though who knows what they will do with your data? You buy a smartphone that integrates everything you like to do on the web. You shop online, unaware that your computer stores information about your purchases that other sites will use to serve you highly-targeted adverts and to adjust their own pricing policies to get you to spend more. It's fast, convenient, and the impacts on your privacy aren't visible at the moment you click.

At this point in time, we have no way of knowing exactly where these changes will lead. We have only lessons from history, the Bible's warnings about the abuses of power, and a small but increasing number of cautionary examples of what happens when our personal data falls into or is placed in the wrong hands. Take the case of the text message received by thousands of Ukrainians on 21 January, 2014: 'Dear subscriber, you have been registered as a participant in a mass disturbance.' The Ukrainian government used mobile phone records to pinpoint the locations of phones in the area around confrontations with riot police earlier that day.[87] In the US, phone tracing is routinely used by the police and other organisations to track people, in both emergencies and non-emergencies, and often with little court oversight.[88] So whilst our destination is still uncertain, the direction of travel is becoming clearer.

TECHNOLOGY AS SALVATION?

Because many of these issues have been raised by the proliferation of communications technology such as the internet, smartphones and social networking, there is also a temptation to see technology

---

87 http://www.nytimes.com/2014/01/22/world/europe/ukraine-protests.html?_r=0
88 http://www.nytimes.com/2012/04/01/us/police-tracking-of-cellphones-raises-privacy-fears.html?pagewanted=all

as the solution. Since the late 1980s the so-called Cypherpunk movement has advocated the use of cryptography – strong encryption of data of all kinds – as a solution to the erosion of privacy and compromises in security. This movement maintains that:

> *Privacy is necessary for an open society in the electronic age ... Privacy in an open society also requires cryptography. If I say something, I want it heard only by those for whom I intend it ... We cannot expect governments, corporations, or other large, faceless organizations to grant us privacy out of their beneficence ... We must defend our own privacy if we expect to have any. We must come together and create systems which allow anonymous transactions to take place. People have been defending their own privacy for centuries with whispers, darkness, envelopes, closed doors, secret handshakes, and couriers. The technologies of the past did not allow for strong privacy, but electronic technologies do ... We know that someone has to write software to defend privacy, and since we can't get privacy unless we all do, we're going to write it ... Our code is free for all to use, worldwide. We don't much care if you don't approve of the software we write. We know that software can't be destroyed and that a widely dispersed system can't be shut down.*[89]

Such technology is extremely useful, in that it serves to prevent certain abuses taking place. In this respect it functions a bit like Old Testament Law. The Law did not force people to do the right thing, it aimed to prevent them from carrying out the worst offences. (Jesus noted that the Law prohibited and punished adultery; it did not prevent lust, the precursor to adultery.) The difference is

---

89   http://www.activism.net/cypherpunk/manifesto.html

that technology protects our privacy by removing the *ability* to snoop, not by providing a deterrent through punishment. As John Gilmore, one of the early advocates for freedom and privacy on the net, said: 'I want a guarantee – with physics and mathematics, not with laws – that we can give ourselves things like real privacy of personal communications. Encryption strong enough that even the NSA can't break it. We already know how. But we're not applying it.' (As it happens, this is a fast-moving area and there is now a deliberate move towards ubiquitous end-to-end encryption, as demonstrated by Apple's stance on the new iPhone. There is thus a constant arms race to discover and exploit new weak points in the process, on the part of the intelligence services, and to prevent unwanted access on the part of the providers and users.)

These approaches are necessary, but they are not sufficient. They address the situation by making certain things impossible or extremely difficult, but they do not get to the root of the issue. Technology can enforce best practices, but it cannot change the attitude of the heart. To use a biblical analogy, it prevents adultery but does not stop lust.

This is important to remember as we look for solutions. It is easy to be apocalyptic about technology – to believe that it is to blame for problems that are really a matter of human nature. But it is also possible to be overly messianic, and claim that it can be used to fix problems that are fundamentally about our relationships with God and with each other. In the worst cases, this may constitute a form of idolatry, worshipping the created order (whether this means the laws of mathematics that protect our communications from unwanted readers, or the devices we build) over the Creator.

WHAT CAN WE DO?

Governments and corporations carry out surveillance of their citizens and users on a staggering scale. Harvesting data from our browsing habits; collecting information from emails, phone calls and text messages, tracking us via smartphones and social networks: all of these and more have become entirely routine. Personal information may be shared with other government or corporate organisations, or unwittingly lost or stolen by cyber criminals. Those under surveillance (all of us) have very little visibility of what is going on, or the use to which this information is put. In many cases, permission has not even been sought to collect this material.

Faced with the seemingly impossible issue of what to do about mass surveillance, many people are content to accept it as the price of living in a hyper-connected world and using the services that businesses offer in return for our personal data. Christians may be more disposed than most people to conclude that if they aren't doing anything wrong, they don't have anything to worry about.

And yet mass surveillance poses an insidious threat to our freedoms and to our faith. On the simplest level, there is the problem that securing the personal data that has been collected is never foolproof, as a number of high-profile hacks have shown, both from government and corporate systems.

From the Bible's perspective there are at least two other major issues. One is that mass surveillance can only be carried out by powerful, centralised authorities that are by their very nature distant and relatively unaccountable for what they are doing, despite the fact that it's supposedly in our interests. Centralised power, whether political, financial or technological, is viewed with extreme suspicion in the Bible, because it tends to be neglectful or abusive of those it is supposed to serve.

This problem goes hand-in-hand with the issue of freedom. We frequently collude with the practices of mass surveillance, because they benefit us in one way or another – most obviously in the case of online services that take our details and track our activity as the price of using them. In doing so, we voluntarily give up information that can be and is used to monitor and control our behaviour, and that of those with whom we associate. If the organisation collecting data is seen as benign, we may not worry too much about the purposes to which the information is being put. However, we cannot assume that they will always remain well-meaning, or that individuals or groups within that organisation might not exploit that knowledge and use it against us.

Whether a government, corporation or individual is responsible, the result is a gradual loss of liberty for us. Reduced autonomy means we are no longer free to act according to conscience. The freedom won for us through Christ's death is compromised by our own actions.

This does not mean that 'Christ died for civil liberties': a straw man that one reader of an early draft of this book raised. 'For Christ also suffered once for sins, the righteous for the unrighteous, to bring you to God' (1 Peter 3:18). However, slavery reduces the freedoms we have to act in accordance with our faith – and thus, apart from any other reasons, we should be careful of giving up those freedoms voluntarily. Whilst in slavery in Egypt, the Israelites were prevented from resting on the Sabbath (Deuteronomy 5:12–15), and they were forbidden from holding a festival to the Lord in the wilderness (Exodus 5:1–5).

This apparently leaves us with a dilemma: do we risk giving up a part of our spiritual freedom, or do we give up our use of these technologies and thereby deny ourselves their own advantages and freedoms, which also has implications for our faith, since they can also be used to such positive effect? Fortunately, this is a false choice: although we may need to be more discerning, we do not need to live as hermits to honour God through our use of technology.

The next chapter looks at the issue of privacy and the personal responses we can make to the issue of mass surveillance.

But Christians should not limit their responses to personal behaviour. When we see injustice around us, it is our duty not only to protect ourselves but to be salt and light for our culture. 'For if you remain silent at this time, relief and deliverance for the Jews will arise from another place, but you and your father's family will perish. And who knows but that you have come to your royal position for such a time as this?' (Esther 4:14).

1. *Support relevant groups.* The secrecy and asymmetry of power that are characteristic of mass surveillance makes it hard to engage directly with the problem as individuals. If you are concerned, you may like to join, support and find out more about privacy and human rights groups active in this area:

   • *Open Rights Group* (www.openrightsgroup.org). ORG works with partners through campaigning, lobbying and legal activity to uphold free expression and privacy, and preserve an open society online. 'We want a society built on laws, free from disproportionate, unaccountable surveillance and censorship. We want a society in which information flows more freely. We want a state that is transparent and accountable, where the public's rights are acknowledged and upheld.'

   • *Electronic Frontier Foundation* (www.eff.org). The US-based EFF is the 'leading nonprofit organisation defending civil liberties in the digital world. Founded in 1990, EFF champions user privacy, free expression, and innovation through impact litigation, policy analysis, grassroots activism, and technology development.'

- *Liberty* (www.liberty-human-rights.org.uk). Liberty 'campaigns for civil liberties and human rights in the UK. Our members have been holding the powerful to account, changing the law and making the news for 80 years.'

2. *Find out more about and review any privacy policies* at your place of work or local church. Are they implemented properly? Is personal data properly secured and protected? These are details that should be available from an organisation's website and be readily available for employees.

3. *Know what information your operating system collects.* Windows harvests large amounts of data by default (especially Windows 10 but also 7 and 8). Microsoft collects information like browser history, user location, calendar records and much more. You can find guides online about how to disable certain settings. Linux does not have the same problem, but is harder to use. Browsers like Firefox, Chrome and Explorer also have privacy settings you should understand and adjust accordingly.

4. *Learn what else is being done with your data.* The same should be the case for the services and outlets you use online – apps you download, e-commerce and other services you use and that require (or take) personal information. What are their policies and track records of protecting customer data? These should be stated up front. A fit-for-purpose privacy statement should make it absolutely clear what information is collected, how it is stored and who has access to it – is it sold to third parties, shared with key business partners, or kept entirely confidential? If details are absent, exercise caution until

you know what the situation is! You will need to be clear what you will tolerate; it is one thing for an organisation to have access to your email address, another for it to have your phone number.

5. *Understand cloud storage.* People routinely store photos, documents and other data on cloud storage platforms. These operate in different ways. Some encrypt your data before it leaves your computer, others on the company's own server (note that this can have implications over who can access your data if you lose your password – if you have sole control over your data, you have sole responsibility for it too!). Some platforms have track records of hacks and lost data.

Employers can read your personal emails. The European Court of Human Rights made the decision that it was acceptable for bosses to spy on employees' messages after a case in which a Romanian engineer took action against his employer after he had been fired for sending messages to his fiancée using a private chat app. The Court ruled against him, saying it was 'not unreasonable for an employer to want to verify that the employees are completing their professional tasks during working hours', and deeming that the surveillance was legitimate. 'The employer had accessed the applicant's Yahoo Messenger account in the belief that it had contained professional messages, since the latter had initially claimed that he had used it in order to advise clients,' the court wrote.

The engineer took the unnamed company to court for invading his privacy; the content of the messages, which 'referred to the sexual health problems affecting the applicant and his fiancée', as well as dealing with 'other personal information, such as his uneasiness with the hostile working environment', were leaked to colleagues before he was fired for using company equipment for personal purposes.[90]

As long as they are transparent about their practices, employers can carry out surveillance on employees throughout the working day. If you access personal accounts – email, instant messaging, social networking – in work time, they have a right to know under the law.

That might be cause for both concern and reflection. On the one hand, there is something uncomfortable about knowing your employer might be, metaphorically, looking over your shoulder the whole time. And on the other hand, how many of us can claim we've always given our paid work 100 per cent of our attention, honouring Paul's words in Ephesians 6:7–8?

'Serve wholeheartedly, as if you were serving the LORD, not

---

90 http://www.wired.co.uk/news/archive/2016-01/13/employers-can-read-your-private-messages

people, because you know that the LORD *will reward each one for whatever good they do, whether they are slave or free.'*[91]
For Christians, then, there is an uncomfortable tension. On the one hand, we ought to be acting in such a way that acknowledges God sees everything, and therefore we have nothing to hide from this kind of surveillance. In practice, our actions frequently belie this principle, suggesting that we don't take God's sovereignty as seriously as we might. And yet even if we are doing the right thing all the time, there is still something unpleasant about being watched – and there are good spiritual and practical reasons to avoid it.

91   This was originally directed at slaves, but holds for any form of employment
      – or any other task we undertake.

7. KEEP OUT!

WHY YOU DON'T JUST CLOSE THE DOOR
BECAUSE YOU HAVE SOMETHING TO HIDE

A couple of years ago I found an iPhone that someone had dropped in the snow on the path, on my way to work. I handed it in to a nearby coffee shop in the hope that the owner would collect it, but ten days later no one had claimed it so they gave it back to me. The phone was locked with its pin code and I couldn't access the address book to look at any contacts who might help me return it. I learned that holding down the 'home' button still worked and enabled voice dialling. (As it happens, I also learned I could download a piece of free software that would crack the pin within a few minutes – this was before Apple included its auto-delete function.) The instruction 'Call Dad' brought up the name and number of the phone owner's father. I left a message but initially there was no response. Using his name, though, it was a straightforward matter to search online and learn his job, his wife and children's names, the church they attended, their social media profiles, photos, hobbies – even their home address. The father was pleased to receive his daughter's phone back – he kindly gave me a bottle of wine as a thank you. Perhaps he would have been more concerned about the family's online security if he'd known how easy it was to track them. That was just one person with benign intentions, using nothing more than Google.

The last chapter discussed the rise of mass surveillance, mainly by states and large corporations, but also by individuals and groups who either carry it out themselves or gain access to data gathered by others. This chapter looks further at the personal effects of our loss of privacy, and the responses that we can make to this as individuals.

PRIVACY VS ANONYMITY

Firstly, it's useful to understand the difference between privacy and anonymity – two related but distinct ideas.

- *Privacy* is the ability to do something away from the eyes of others, such as closing the curtains at home or holding a private conversation with another person. Everyone has some need for privacy, and this usually has nothing to do with illegal activity. Few people have a lock on their bathroom door because they are plotting to overthrow the government from the privacy of their shower.

- *Anonymity* means being able to do something visibly and publicly, but without people knowing *who* is doing it. Voting, whistle-blowing and paying for something in cash are examples of anonymity. Like privacy, anonymity in itself does not indicate unethical or illegal activity. Sending your letter in an unmarked envelope does not indicate a treasonous conspiracy with the recipient, for example.

Of course, if we are to enjoy the benefits and protections that society offers then there are compromises we have to make. Privacy and anonymity have to be balanced with our need for **security**. If a terrorist cell is planning an attack, we want the tools and abilities to stop them. Clearly, both privacy and anonymity make this harder.

Nevertheless, these basic examples show that the need for privacy and anonymity are deeply rooted in human nature. They are, to borrow language from the United States Declaration of Independence, self-evident truths. They are values that run to the heart of a free and democratic society, which is why the right to privacy, within reasonable boundaries, is stated in the Universal Declaration of Human Rights: 'No one shall be subjected to arbitrary interference with his privacy, family, home or correspondence, nor to attacks upon his honour and reputation. Everyone has the right to the protection of the law against such interference or attacks' (Article 12).

HOW DO WE REACT?

Most of us know a little about the routine collection of our personal data, but fewer do anything about it. Sharing information is how we sign up to services online. Web apps don't tend to require a financial subscription any more: the cost we pay is our personal details, which are valuable to the company because they can use them to target advertising (and sometimes sell on to others). It's the price of doing business. In any case, there's a good chance we're giving away large amounts of information on social media anyway. Often this is entirely unnecessary. Facebook doesn't need to know your birthday, but it asks for it anyway.

It's worth noting the asymmetry of power in this process. Typically, you don't get to have much of a say in what you share. The deal is that you provide the information 'requested' or you don't get to use the service. The Terms and Conditions that you probably skimmed at best don't allow any negotiation, yet they imply a contractual relationship. The customer is at a disadvantage, since engaging with a large company over the internet is extremely difficult, and they are hardly likely to tailor their terms just for you – though previous cases about privacy settings and other issues have shown that Facebook and others do respond if there is pressure from enough people. And there are limits to the liberties companies can take and enforce in their online terms, as recent court cases have shown.[92] All the same, the customer typically has little power over what they submit in return for using the application, and little visibility over how these details are stored and used.

Generally, the main reason we try to maintain any kind of online security or take any level of care about the personal information we allow to be made public is because we don't want to be the victim of a hack or identity theft. Even that may be little more than an inconvenience. We know that if a hacker steals our identity or credit card details, the banks or credit card companies will cover our losses, unless we have been demonstrably careless.

And yet, many of us still experience a profound uneasiness about the fact we are being watched, with almost literally our every move – online and off – being tracked. Research in 2014 showed that '91% of American adults say that consumers have lost control over how personal information is collected and used by companies'.[93] The public has little confidence in the security of their everyday communications, and some 80 per cent are concerned about the level of government surveillance.[94]

One of the problems is that we are often uncertain of how to react. These are large, powerful organisations, and engaging with them directly is typically ineffective. Additionally, some of the surveillance is done in the name of our own freedom, and with judicial oversight. Even if we are worried about intrusive surveillance by governments, we might accept it as the price we pay to keep us safe from terrorist attacks and organised crime.

We often justify these means to ourselves on the grounds that if you're not doing anything wrong, you don't have anything to worry

---

92 See http://www.forbes.com/sites/ericgoldman/2012/10/10/how-zappos-user-agreement-failed-in-court-and-left-zappos-legally-naked/#2359bf192f6b

93 http://www.pewresearch.org/key-data-points/privacy/

94 http://www.bbc.co.uk/news/technology-30004304

about. Perhaps Christians, already used to the idea of an unseen but all-seeing presence, are even less concerned than others. But even if we did accept that government surveillance at its current level was necessary – which is far from a given – they are not the only ones watching us and there are lots of unintended consequences to deal with.

PRIVACY AND CONSUMERISM

Companies and other organisations routinely track our movements online. This behaviour is extensive across the web and can easily be uncovered.

Chances are, you visit a huge array of different websites every day. What you might not know is that while you do that, there is an 'invisible web' at work: companies are following your activities, collecting your data, and using it in various ways. They do it through technology known as 'trackers'.

There are thousands of such trackers from different companies, and they are active all the time, even though you don't see their activity and may not be aware of what's happening. This is true on the websites you visit from desktop or laptop computers, and on mobile apps as well.

Trackers are neither inherently good nor inherently bad – they are a fact of life and their purposes vary widely, from the helpful to the potentially creepy. Some of them allow you to customize your experience on the websites you frequent and they recognize you when you return to favorite sites. Ever have the experience of visiting a website and then seeing ads for that business show up everywhere you go afterward? That's because of trackers. And, behind the scenes, trackers build profiles of users' web behavior, data which is regularly sold to companies you may have never heard of.[95]

I installed the Ghostery browser extension to see how different sites tracked me. The BBC website showed up 4 trackers, 3 advertising-related and one for analytics. Facebook, unexpectedly, had only one. Christianity.com had a rather surprising 20, mostly for advertising. Amazon.com, 5; eBay, 8. Wondering about examples that could provide useful leads for business, I checked a series of popular song lyrics sites. One showed 47 trackers, another 24, another 28. A popular film reviews site, 40. One tabloid newspaper site, 46; another, 22; a third, 23. Google and Wikipedia had none. What quickly becomes clear is that a large proportion of the sites you visit are collecting information about your browsing habits. Some sites – especially news sites – will even refuse you access if you are running anti-tracker software.

Many of us feel uncomfortable about the idea we're being tracked, even if we are doing nothing wrong. We have already discussed the problem that giving up agency over our lives and habits can reduce our freedoms to act in a way aligned with our faith. The Always-On culture reduces our ability to concentrate, for example, posing many distractions to our faith and relationships. Allowing our every action to be tracked similarly gives power over us to a third party.

One obvious impact of this harvesting of personal details by websites and companies is that it facilitates the consumerism that permeates our lives. The adverts we receive are highly targeted, because they are personalised campaigns created from our previous browsing activities. Thus there is the two-edged sword of being served adverts that cater precisely to our personal interests. Treated with caution, this is useful, filtering out irrelevant material; you can argue that if you are going to be served with adverts at all, you might as well be served with ones that could be of relevance to you.

---

95 https://www.ghostery.com/why-ghostery/tracker-basics/

On the other hand, consumerism's tendency to encourage us to create a world in our own image has serious implications for our faith, as well as our bank balances.

In other instances, maintaining privacy is a matter of security and safety – ours and other people's. The more personal information that is available about you, the easier it is for criminals to gain your trust or access to your accounts, and potentially other people's, too. As we explored in the chapter on identity, this has a range of unanticipated spiritual implications.

PRIVACY, DIGNITY AND AUTONOMY

Companies are not the only ones to monitor our behaviour online, ubiquitous though this practice is. Governments also collect large amounts of data about their citizens. The nature of mass surveillance is that the security services do not 'tap' a particular individual, like the old spy movies where it's possible to listen in on a phone conversation by connecting crocodile clips to the right terminals. They collect everything, and then filter it for key words and other information that *might* indicate someone is up to no good. In the course of researching this book, I carried out numerous searches to learn more about Tor, an application that allows anonymous web browsing. Although I am not planning to carry out a terrorist attack or commit any form of organised (or disorganised) crime,[96] this will have prompted a red flag. Knowing this made me wary of carrying out further such searches (and, indeed, I occasionally used Tor to make them).

Was this a good thing? The fact that I know I'm being watched means I am less likely to act illegally or unethically. Arguably, this is positive: it makes the world a safer place. But does it make it a more *godly* place? I would argue not.

---

96 I know I wouldn't admit it in a book if I was. But I'm still not.

Free will is fundamental to our faith. This idea is a critical element of some theodicies that seek to explain the presence of evil in the world created by a loving God. God could have created us as robots who had no choice but to follow him, but that would have rendered our faith meaningless. Instead, he gave us free choice to love him or not. In doing so, he also made us capable of sin.

Arguably, religious freedom depends on the freedom to be able to sin as well as to avoid sin. The Vatican's Declaration on Religious Freedom reads, 'the human person has a right to religious freedom. This freedom means that all men are to be immune from coercion on the part of individuals or of social groups and of any human power, in such wise that no one is to be forced to act in a manner contrary to his own beliefs, whether privately or publicly, whether alone or in association with others, within due limits.'[97] If I avoid doing something wrong because I am scared of the consequences, rather than because I believe it to be wrong and want to honour God by my actions, then my decision is less meaningful.

In practice, we often avoid sin or crime because we are aware of the consequences. The social contract we implicitly hold with those around us involves giving up the ability to act precisely as we want in return for the protections of living together. Oscar Wilde famously wrote, 'Conscience and cowardice are really the same things, Basil. Conscience is the trade-name of the firm. That is all.'[98] But the sheer extent of surveillance means there is little that falls outside of the knowledge of the authorities. The knowledge that we are being watched and tracked undermines human dignity. In the words of one writer, 'Christians should desire and help create a society where the tendency of citizens is to look up, not over their shoulders.'[99]

---

97 http://www.vatican.va/archive/hist_councils/ii_vatican_council/ documents/vat-ii_decl_19651207_dignitatis-humanae_en.html

98 Oscar Wilde, *The Picture of Dorian Gray* (1890).

99 Jonathan Merritt, see http://jonathanmerritt.religionnews.com/2013/ 07/04/should-christians-oppose-the-surveillance-state/

WILLING SLAVES

When Jesus is asked whether it is right to pay taxes to Caesar, he tells them to bring him a denarius and asks them whose portrait and inscription are on the coin. "'Caesar's,' they replied. Then Jesus said to them, "Give back to Caesar what is Caesar's and to God what is God's'" (Mark 12:16–17). Paul reiterates that we are to obey earthly authorities. 'Give to everyone what you owe them: If you owe taxes, pay taxes; if revenue, then revenue; if respect, then respect; if honour, then honor' (Romans 13:7).

This obedience to the state is necessary but limited: it is not to conflict with our loyalty to God, and neither are we to stay quiet in the face of injustice. The prophets were outspoken against Israel's kings for their idolatry and foreign policy, and against the wealthy classes for their treatment of the poor. The early Christians were persecuted by the Romans because they placed faith in God above allegiance to Caesar. In Acts 4, Peter and John are arrested by the Jewish authorities after they preach in the Temple grounds. 'They called them in again and commanded them not to speak or teach at all in the name of Jesus. But Peter and John replied, "Which is right in God's eyes: to listen to you, or to him? You be the judges! As for us, we cannot help speaking about what we have seen and heard."'

And thus, the question raised for us by mass surveillance is: Does this, in principle or in practice, compromise my ability to act in accordance with my faith? Does a loss of privacy reduce the choices I have to express my faith?

This is one danger posed to our faith by mass surveillance. It is one that may be more acute in oppressive regimes such as China and Iran, but we should also be aware of the risks in the West. When we do not resist the loss of privacy – due to government or corporate surveillance – we allow Caesar to take the place of God. We implicitly say that we don't really care about our autonomy, that the right to browse the web and communicate with each other and access information is more important than our own freedom.

Every concession we make, actively or otherwise, makes us slightly less human – because as Christians, our understanding of humanity is informed by the price Jesus paid for us on the cross.

Once we are informed about the level of surveillance routinely undertaken, the concessions we make suggest where our priorities lie. There are two competing freedoms from which to choose, or more accurately a path between them we need to negotiate. There are the very real freedoms of access to knowledge and empowerment, but this can be taken at the expense of freedoms to our faith.

The data harvested by mass surveillance is personal. Often, we do not even give our explicit consent for it to be taken, or we give it up lightly (those T&Cs no one really reads …). It's a little like Esau selling his birthright for a bowl of stew (Genesis 27). That data *may* be used to predict a terrorist attack. Far more routinely, it may be used to predict where we are going, who we are meeting, the products we consume and services we purchase. Intervention in any of these areas compromises our autonomy. Our ability to direct our paths towards God's kingdom becomes a step further away each time. And unfortunately, it is impossible to give the ability to intercept and store data to only one party (assuming we'd want to), without also giving others the ability to do the same. This is the argument behind Apple's decision to contest the FBI's request to put a back door in the iPhone: a feature or vulnerability that lets the security services access data also opens the possibility of hackers, criminals and rogue states doing the same.

WHAT CAN WE DO ABOUT IT?

There was of course no way of knowing whether you were being watched at any given moment. How often, or on what system, the Thought Police plugged in on any individual wire was guesswork. It was even conceivable that they watched everybody all the time. But at any rate they could plug in your wire whenever they wanted to. You had to live – did live, from habit that became instinct – in the assumption that every sound you made was overheard, and, except in darkness, every movement scrutinized.

GEORGE ORWELL, *1984*[100]

George Orwell's classic novel of the totalitarian surveillance state was written almost seventy years ago but its themes have continuing relevance given the ongoing debate about the infringement of privacy carried out by state and corporate organisations. These raise the question of what we can actually do. In *1984*, Winston Smith is depicted as an insignificant part of a huge and powerful state apparatus, unable to resist its will without bring crushed. In our case, the distance between individuals and those who collect data on us, their anonymity and lack of accountability – the very reasons the Bible is wary of such concentrations of power – also makes it extremely difficult to address the problem.

Additionally, for Christians, there is the biblical principle of submitting to authority, so long as this does not conflict with our loyalty to God. In Romans 13 Paul makes it clear that Christians are to try, wherever possible, to get along with our earthly rulers, who have been established by God. We may not break laws just because we don't like them.

Let everyone be subject to the governing authorities, for there is no authority except that which God has established. The authorities that exist have been established by God. Consequently, whoever rebels against the authority is rebelling against what God has instituted, and those who do so will bring judgment on themselves. For rulers hold no terror for those who do

100 George Orwell, *1984* (Secker & Warburg, 1949).

right, but for those who do wrong. Do you want to be free from fear of the one in authority? Then do what is right and you will be commended. For the one in authority is God's servant for your good. But if you do wrong, be afraid, for rulers do not bear the sword for no reason. They are God's servants, agents of wrath to bring punishment on the wrongdoer. Therefore, it is necessary to submit to the authorities, not only because of possible punishment but also as a matter of conscience.

ROMANS 13:1–5

At the same time, we must also resist evil and stand up for those who are vulnerable. As Jesus says in Mark 12, we are to give to Caesar what is Caesar's, and to God what is God's. This placed the burden of deciding what was legitimately Caesar's and what was owed to God on his listeners. The decision as to where we draw the line and refuse to obey the state must not be taken lightly. Neither, of course, can our resolution to obey God first.

PERSONAL RESPONSIBILITY

Aside from taking steps to prevent unwanted onlookers, we need to be more careful about what we intentionally or inadvertently make public. It makes little sense to complain about intrusive surveillance when we are giving away much of the same information through our social media profiles. This information is a gift to anyone who wants to track us, for any reason.

Finally, there are risks that come with the ability to avoid identification. Being able to act without fear of being tracked and monitored is an important freedom – and arguably one that makes our decisions more meaningful, because they are not taken in a climate of fear. However, increased privacy raises the question of what we do with that freedom: what you do in private is arguably more indicative of your true character than how you act when you know you are being watched.

There are many warnings in the Bible of sins committed in secret that are seen by God and that will be made known. 'There is nothing concealed that will not be disclosed, or hidden that will not be made known. What you have said in the dark will be heard in the daylight, and what you have whispered in the ear in the inner rooms will be proclaimed from the roofs' (Luke 12:2–3). The internet is a source of many temptations of all kinds, some of which will be explored in the next chapter, and greater anonymity can be a catalyst to explore these. It is interesting that Jesus follows his warning on secret sin with another: 'I tell you, my friends, do not be afraid of those who kill the body and after that can do no more. But I will show you whom you should fear: Fear him who, after your body has been killed, has authority to throw you into hell. Yes, I tell you, fear him.' This could almost be written for the debate around privacy and surveillance: in seeking to escape one evil, we must be careful not to be ensnared by a worse one.

Grappling with the issues raised by mass surveillance and the erosion of privacy can be overwhelming. By its nature, this is something that affects every area of life and occurs all around us, every day.

We should assume, for starters, that just about all of our communications are monitored and almost everything we do online is tracked, unless we take specific steps to avoid this. This includes government agencies like the NSA and GCHQ, which have access to emails and phone records. It is worth stating that the greater the effort you make to avoid surveillance, the closer the scrutiny you are likely to attract.

Computer code leaked from the NSA suggests that people who search for certain software that enables them to use the web more anonymously are flagged for further attention – or even those who visit sites that have a broad interest in online privacy.[101] However, we must remember that this also includes corporations that record our browsing habits for commercial gain, as well as individuals who gain access to your computer through a wide variety of means to use it and your email and social media accounts for their own ends.

The common argument that 'If you're not doing anything wrong, you don't have anything to worry about' does not hold true. Even if the organisation collecting the data is doing so for a legitimate reason and with our consent, there is always scope for others to access it. For Christians, this should serve as a reminder that God sees everything and judges justly. 'For there is nothing hidden that will not be disclosed, and nothing concealed that will not be known or brought out into the open' (Luke 8:17).

1. *Don't trust others to keep your details secure.* Companies may be unwilling or unable to keep your data safe. It is best not left to chance! Aside from keeping best practices online, there are various applications that can help you. Some of the software that enables you to protect your privacy is still rather technical, and not suitable for most casual users. Other programmes are simple enough that anyone can use them with little extra effort.

   • *Email encryption*, for example, comes in various forms, and depending on your email provider can be relatively straightforward to set up. It does require that both sender and recipient use it, though, making it impractical for many day-to-day purposes.

---

101 http://www.theregister.co.uk/2014/07/03/nsa_xkeyscore_stasi_scandal/

- *The Tor Browser* enables anonymous web browsing. Tor (the name comes from the original project title, The Onion Router) was originally developed by the US Naval Research Laboratory to protect online intelligence communications. It works by encrypting web traffic in many layers, like an onion, and routing it through a string of randomly-selected relays, decrypting one layer at each stage. This makes it almost impossible for even the most well-resourced organisations to monitor web traffic. Tor is used by a wide variety of people who are concerned about internet privacy for one reason or another, including journalists and bloggers in oppressive regimes; whistle-blowers; military professionals; victims of domestic violence and stalking, and those who work with them; and individuals concerned about the erosion of privacy and the rise of online surveillance. Despite its many legitimate purposes, most of the news coverage around Tor describes its use by criminals for various illegal activities. Tor offers robust privacy but is slower than a regular browser due to the circuitous route the data takes to its destination.

  Tor hides the very worst of everything available on the web. *Tor hidden services* are websites only reachable through Tor. Although they include some legitimate and hobbyist sites, the vast majority are dedicated to illegal activity, from drugs and weapons sales to illegal pornography, credit card fraud and even murder for hire. For most Christian users, Tor offers greater security than they would reasonably need. In *some* cases, there may be good reason to use it for browsing the Clearnet (the regular web). There will seldom, if ever, be a legitimate reason for using the dark web. There is also the likelihood that using Tor or even searching for information about it will flag you for further attention by the authorities.

- *Search engine Duckduckgo.com* is designed to protect users' privacy and provide objective search results that are not based on profiling (as traditional commercial search engines do – the results you see are tailored to individuals' accounts and web histories). In contrast to the bigger commercial players, they have a no-tracking policy and provide clear, uncluttered results.

- *Startpage.com* uses Google search results, but without logging information about you. The nature of these resources is that the best option can change quickly as new services come online and old ones are discontinued, so it is worth searching for other ones.

2. *Choosing and remembering strong passwords* is a small price to pay for maintaining our online privacy and autonomy. If you need help generating and remembering secure passwords, there are plenty of resources to help you online.[102] Writing passwords down is not as dangerous as many people assume: few housebreakers are after such information. Reusing passwords is a bad idea, since if one becomes known, several other accounts may be compromised. If you are going to reuse passwords, do so judiciously: for example, do not use the same password to log in to online banking that you also use for your main email account, which is used to verify changes for your online banking account!

3. *Check your privacy settings.* Many of us simply don't care enough about our privacy to take the trouble to

---

102 E.g. http://lifehacker.com/four-methods-to-create-a-secure-password-youll-actually-1601854240

adjust our social media settings to prevent others from learning details about us that we would prefer remain personal. This typically takes just a few minutes to research and fix, if it is an issue. We are too ready to give our details away in return for signing up to particular services online – and all too often, we'll use the same password for the service as for the email address we use to sign up with.

4. *Install an ad blocker.* If you want to browse the web without being inundated with adverts – which can contain trackers and malware, as well as being annoying and slowing your computer down – you can install a piece of software to block them. These are generally configurable to filter out adverts according to the criteria you set. There are many options but one of the most popular is AdBlock Plus.[103] The Ghostery plug-in will also inform you of how many trackers are on each site you visit.[104]

---

103 https://adblockplus.org
104 https://www.ghostery.com/

I'm a member of a few online communities and they can display the best and the worst of human nature. The nature of these communities is that people don't tend to use their real names or disclose much information about their offline identities, unless they really need to for one reason or another. Partly it's convention and partly it's because the internet is full of some pretty strange people and there are plenty of horror stories of users being cyber-stalked or 'doxxed' – where somebody maliciously gathers information about you and then dumps it publicly for everyone to see. The anonymity means that people trade on their reputation, rather than social status or qualifications.

In one community there was a long-term member who needed money because he had to go into hospital. He had been around almost since the beginning of the community, and had contributed a lot in terms of time, expertise and effort, as well as his personal resources.

He didn't give details about the treatment he needed, but he wasn't asking for donations – he offered to sell a number of things to raise the $8,000 he needed. He was somewhat desperate as time was short, and he was selling at below market price. Still, he had trouble raising the amount he needed.

Then one day, shortly before he was due to go into hospital, he received a gift. Someone had sent him the equivalent of $9,000 in virtual currency. No one knew who the donor was, and he never came forwards to say who he was or even that he had made the transfer. He just saw the guy's post on the forum and sent the money. The recipient was, to say the least, surprised and delighted.

The bottom line: no one had met either of them in real life. Someone who held money lightly, and who didn't seek any kind of recognition or thanks, sent a large sum to someone who needed it – despite the fact he didn't know so much as his real name. There's no indication of whether the donor has any kind of faith, but in terms of using anonymity well, that's a tough example to beat.

8. YOU CAN, THEREFORE YOU SHOULD

HOW BEING ABLE TO DO ANYTHING MEANS WE'RE TEMPTED BY EVERYTHING

Millions of football fans view it as a victimless crime. Subscriptions to sports services are expensive, so instead they turn to illegal sites that offer free streams of popular matches. There are thousands of such pirate sites and their business model is to pull in revenues from advertising. Naturally, few mainstream brands want to be associated with such illegal activity – to call a spade a spade, it's theft – and so the sites' hosts turn to less reputable sources. Through a variety of techniques, often surreptitiously delivered through these adverts and downloads the sites say are required to watch a game, the majority of the services install malicious software on your computer.[105]

Moreover, the malware can have far-reaching effects. 'You have to install the extension, and once the user installs the extensions, it can infect any website the user is visiting,' one researcher told the BBC. 'So, if a person installs an extension to watch a stream, and then visits a site like BBC.com, this extension can actually change the contents of BBC.com as it appears in the user's browser so that it includes malicious links and advertising. This is extremely dangerous.'

---

105 http://www.bbc.co.uk/news/technology-35434765

It is very hard to prevent this kind of piracy, because even if one site is shut down the hosts can move their stream to another. There are many companies that will offer no-questions-asked hosting for just about any kind of business, legitimate or otherwise, and taking legal action against them can be almost impossible due to their relative anonymity and location in jurisdictions beyond the reach of the authorities.

The anonymity of the web means many are tempted to visit these sites in the interests of saving a few pounds to watch a match. Aside from the moral issue, there is the very real likelihood of having your privacy compromised and personal data stolen. (It turns out there really is no honour among thieves.) Individual users will probably not be caught by the authorities, though this does not mean it is consequence-free. For the Christian, the ultimate question that the anonymity of the web and our access to these and other services raises concerns how we use our freedom – and whether that expression of freedom means we really can be called free.

As argued in the very first chapter, every new technology involves a shift in power because it gives an advantage to those who use it. The rapid growth and availability of communications technologies represents just such a shift in power. It hands us new capabilities – and with them, new freedoms and responsibilities. There are both huge advantages and huge pitfalls, and we cannot have the one without the other.

FREEDOM OF SPEECH

Take, for example, the role played by social media and instant messaging for freedom of speech, or simply for learning what is going on around the world. Access to information is critical for justice and democracy. Technology helps us cut through the propaganda, or at least to find different opinions and make up our own minds.

Smartphones and instant messaging played a pivotal role in the Arab Spring: the series of popular uprisings against oppressive states that began in December 2010 in Tunisia and spread to several other nations in the Arab world. Although many of these effectively failed in the long term, as one repressive regime was replaced by another, it was the ability to share information quickly with large numbers of people that allowed citizens to take action they would never have been able to ten years earlier – and to ensure the rest of the world knew what was happening. It is telling that the authorities tried to prevent demonstrations by shutting down internet access.

Being capable of sharing an immense amount of uncensored and accurate information throughout social networking sites has contributed to the cause of many Arab Spring activists. Through social networking sites, Arab Spring activists have not only gained the power to overthrow powerful dictatorships, but also helped Arab civilians become aware of the underground communities that exist and are made up of their brothers, and others willing to listen to their stories.

In countries like Egypt, Tunisia, and Yemen, rising action plans such as protests made up of thousands, have been organized through social media such as Facebook and Twitter. 'We use Facebook to schedule the protests' an Arab Spring activist from Egypt announced 'and [we use] Twitter to coordinate, and YouTube to tell the world.' The role that technology has taken in allowing the distribution of public information such as the kinds stated by the aforementioned activist, had been essential in establishing the democratic movement that has helped guide abused civilians to overthrow their oppressor.[106]

Democracy must be built through open societies that share information. When there is information, there is enlightenment. When there is debate, there are solutions. When there is no sharing of power, no rule of law, no accountability, there is abuse, corruption, subjugation and indignation.

ATIFETE JAHJAGA, FORMER PRESIDENT OF KOSOVO

The web therefore has a critical place in making the truth available. Ten or twenty years ago, we might have heard little about what was going on in Tunisia or the Middle East – or received a version of events that was heavily filtered by the interests of those who reported it. Something similar happened with the printing press in the fifteenth and sixteenth centuries: ideas were suddenly available to the public in ways they had never been before. It redistributed power – the ability to read, interpret and apply the Bible's teachings – from a small elite of priests into the hands of ordinary people. This was incredibly inflammatory, because it conflicted with the vested interests of a powerful minority. The printing press played a major role in the Reformation as translations of the Bible and pamphlets containing new ideas became affordable and accessible. The internet heralds a similar shift, bringing a greater democratisation of knowledge. Information is no longer controlled or distributed by professionals and elites. It can be accessed by anyone with a computer and internet connection.

In societies that are not open and where the press and information are largely controlled by the authorities, the freedom offered by technology is immensely valuable. International comment and pressure concerning the treatment of migrant workers in certain

---

106 http://mic.com/articles/10642/twitter-revolution-how-the-arab-spring-was-helped-by-social-media

countries is the only thing that typically makes a difference to the situation, albeit slowly. A free international press is absolutely vital for these kinds of basic justices.

In the UK, we also rely on a free press and freedom of speech to address injustice. Many serious issues have been brought to light by whistle-blowers who have spoken out publicly or anonymously using the internet. Even where their identities are known, the web gives them not only a platform to communicate their message to a large number of people, but safeguards in that the awareness of so many people brings a degree of accountability to the organisations involved.

> *The control of information is something the elite always does, particularly in a despotic form of government. Information, knowledge, is power. If you can control information, you can control people.*
>
> TOM CLANCY, ESPIONAGE NOVELIST

Whistle-blowers are something akin to modern-day prophets, speaking truth to power and bringing into the open injustices which might have remained hidden as those such as Elijah, Isaiah and Amos did. Christians must support such prophetic action and the calling to account of otherwise unaccountable power.

CONSUMER MORALITY

As we explored in earlier chapters, the anonymity of the web can prompt us to act in very different ways to how we do in the rest of life. We often try to compartmentalise our online and offline identities, without grasping that things are not so neat and simple in practice. The 'freedom' we experience through our online anonymity is not something we can expect to switch on and off at will, though it may seem that way. Like the skylark in G H Charnley's children's tale, many people have found that minor compromises can have long-term consequences as they open a door to a new pattern of behaviour that is very hard to escape.

Consumerism makes choice and change the highest good, telling us that through consumption we can be whoever we want to be. The internet makes available to us almost anything we could want, providing the means by which we exercise our rights as consumers.

Morality in a consumer culture is, like everything else, me-shaped. The question becomes not one of 'how does this affect other people?' but 'how does this serve my needs?' In our seemingly anonymous, personally-tailored internet worlds, it is easy to ignore everything else and focus only on what works for us. The typical vices of the web – including illegal file sharing, gambling and pornography, amongst others – are often justified as victimless crimes. Consumerism breeds an attitude of 'If I *can* do it, it's OK', and the lack of detection tends to legitimise that. Of course, no supposedly secret sin is hidden from God, and many people have been surprised when their online behaviour was exposed to the world.

ILLEGAL FILE SHARING

Online piracy is possibly the most popular 'victimless crime' of the web. Piracy had, of course, been around for a long time before the web. It was always possible to copy music and software, even in the days when these were stored on tapes and floppy disks. But as internet connections became faster and the web began to hit critical mass around the turn of the millennium, new services became available through which users could share files directly with each other on an industrial scale. Suddenly, you didn't need to know someone personally who had the music track or video you wanted, and you didn't need to put a physical medium like a CD in the same room as a device to copy it – you could just download a piece of software that would enable you to connect with everyone else who had that software, and access all the files they were making available. Piracy became extremely easy.

Many of the people who used these services – first Napster and now, more sophisticated platforms like BitTorrent, which is fully decentralised and cannot easily be shut down[107] – simply ignored the copyright violations that sharing music and videos often involved. The mentality was that they weren't harming anyone, and they wouldn't otherwise be buying the music, so they weren't costing anyone any money. There is even a movement that claims that information data should always be free, and that the music companies were the ones in the wrong for trying to force people to pay for it. Others recognised that what they were doing was illegal, but the risk of being caught was so low that they just discounted it. Recent cases have shown that this was not true, with high-profile cases in which people have been fined large amounts of money for sharing just a few tracks.[108]

People often justify illegal file sharing on the grounds that it is a victimless crime – perhaps because the only ones to lose out are the wealthy music companies. Christians, especially young people, seem to be just as happy to download copyrighted files as their non-Christian peers. Hillsong, the Australian Pentecostal megachurch well-known for its music label, has lobbied the Australian government to help them stop people from copying their material, which is some of the most pirated in the country.[109]

---

107 The original Napster employed a central server to index all the users online at any given time, and therefore had a single point of failure (SPoF) which enabled the authorities to shut it down. Later file-sharing networks use distributed hash tables (DHTs) to avoid this issue and enable full peer-to-peer communication.

108 See, e.g., http://www.wired.com/2012/05/supreme-court-file-sharing/

109 See http://www.aph.gov.au/Parliamentary_Business/Committees/Senate/ Legal_and_Constitutional_Affairs/Copyright_Bill_2015/Submissions

The various justifications given for illegal file sharing are just that: justifications. The irreducible reality is that something is being sold, for profit, for the benefit of an industry as a whole, for the musicians and artists involved and all the people who work for that company and their families – and other people are taking it for free. Sometimes things are as simple as they seem. There are warnings in the New Testament about submitting to the laws of the country in which we are based (e.g. Romans 13:1), which vary from jurisdiction to jurisdiction, but the basic principle at stake is the eighth commandment: Do not steal.

GAMBLING

Next up in the list of vices comes gambling. It's one that many Christians might overlook as a risk to them personally. Gambling does not occupy the same place in our national consciousness that other vices like alcohol and drug abuse do, despite the damage it can cause. But we would be wrong to ignore it. Around two thirds of people in the UK have gambled in the last year, or just under half, if the National Lottery is excluded.[110] Online gambling is still a relatively small niche, but is highly likely to grow rapidly due to its convenience and availability, and the degree of anonymity that the internet brings. Although gambling is an occasional thing for many people, there are an estimated 350,000 problem gamblers in the UK.[111] Another survey suggests the number may be 450,000, with an average debt of £17,500, and there could be another 900,000 people at 'moderate risk' of becoming problem gamblers.[112] It is inconceivable that many Christians would not be included in these numbers.

---

110 http://www.theguardian.com/news/datablog/2013/dec/19/gambling-health-survey-england-key-statistics
111 http://gamblingaddiction.org.uk/
112 http://www.care.org.uk/our-causes/more/gambling

The Bible says nothing directly about gambling, but many passages point to the dangers. We are warned of the love of money (1 Timothy 6:10) and the lure of getting rich quickly (Proverbs 13:11; Ecclesiastes 5:10). There's the question of stewardship, of wasting money we could be spending more productively – the same may go for many other things on which we spend money; it is not, as Proverbs would put it, wise behaviour.

Ultimately, though, the issue is again one of mastery. Gambling is addictive, or at least compulsive. Often it is those who can least afford it who are attracted by the idea of 'easy' money.

The same goes for some forms of financial speculation, which are really little more than gambling due to the level of risk they entail (binary options and day-trading being two examples – in most cases there is little skill involved). Figures from brokers suggest that 80 per cent of day-traders quit within two years and only a tiny minority consistently make money. Even if trading (or gambling) is successful, it sits uncomfortably with the Christian faith. Most forms of speculation look to gain something for nothing, making money from the movements of the markets rather than in productive activity. Relationally, trading is problematic since every successful day-trader 'earns' money at the expense of another, who loses it. The purpose of trading is to saddle someone else with a stock or commodity you believe will lose value.[113]

PORNOGRAPHY

Pornography use and addiction is a serious and growing problem for our hyper-connected society, including for Christians. Reliable and up-to-date statistics are hard to find, but it seems that around

---

113   See Paul Mills, 'Investing as a Christian: Reaping where you have not sown'. Cambridge Papers vol. 5 no. 2, 1996. http://www.jubilee-centre.org/investing-as-a-christian-reaping-where-you-have-not-sown-by-paul-mills/

two-thirds of Christian men and one in seven Christian women watch pornography at least once a month.[114] The vast majority of children have been exposed to pornography, with the median age being just eleven. Children are accessing explicit material earlier and earlier, and learning about sex online.

Pornography consumerises sex, turning it into a commodity to be accessed on the individual's terms, outside of meaningful and healthy relationships. It is anathema to love and intimacy. No wonder that over half of divorce cases involve one party who routinely access pornography online.

A detailed treatment of pornography use and addiction[115] is outside the scope of this book, and it is one of the most recognised and discussed pitfalls of our consumerised and Always-On culture for Christians. Briefly, though, Jesus warned that lust is harmful: it is the attitude that lies behind unfaithfulness. 'I tell you that anyone who looks at a woman lustfully has already committed adultery with her in his heart' (Matthew 5:28). Job states, 'I made a covenant with my eyes not to look lustfully at a young woman' (Job 31:1). And Paul, in 1 Corinthians 6, writes that 'The body, however, is not meant for sexual immorality but for the Lord, and the Lord for the body' (1 Corinthians 6:13). The Greek word translated as 'sexual immorality' is *porneia*, a catch-all term for a wide variety of sexual sins not limited to adultery or sex with prostitutes, even though that was Paul's context here.

Even on the entirely secular level, the harm done by the pornography industry is immense. Trafficking and abuse are rife, sexual violence is routine and even integral to much pornography.[116] A pornographic culture takes a huge toll on marriage and other intimate relationships, setting false standards

---

114   http://www.covenanteyes.com/pornstats/
115   Experts differ on whether pornography use can be compared to other addictions like drugs and alcohol. http://www.bbc.co.uk/news/blogs-trending-35651737
116   http://www.covenanteyes.com/2015/11/13/porn-and-sexual-violence-10-facts-from-the-experts/

for what is considered acceptable and normal. As author Wendy Shalit argues, the pornographic society is one in which infidelity is normal.[117]

The vices that the internet opens to us and catalyses are numerous, but common to all of them are the relative anonymity the web offers. This allows us to hide behind a screen and, we believe, escape the consequences of actions we would not want publicly known. Lack of detection or apparent real-world impact legitimises these, suggesting the idea of a 'victimless crime'. However, many or all of these practices are habitual or even addictive, and as such they imprint themselves on our minds and characters. Once again, there is the issue of giving power over minds and souls to someone or something else: 'I will not be mastered by anything'.

1. *Accountability is critical.* Removing the anonymity of the web undermines the power of its temptations. Software like Covenant Eyes,[118] which is targeted at pornography, offers filtering of web content and accountability reports that can be customised according to age and content, and sent to specific accountability partners. Realistically, though, tech-savvy web users can generally find ways around restrictions, so it is also important to have people with whom you can have honest and confidential discussions.

---

117   Wendy Shalit, *A Return to Modesty: Discovering the Lost Virtue* (Free Press, 2000), p. 54.
118   http://www.covenanteyes.com/

2. *'If your hand or your foot causes you to stumble, cut it off ...'* (Matthew 18:8). There is endless debate about whether Jesus was speaking literally here. Assuming you are not actually prepared to contemplate amputation,[119] there is still the figurative solution to harmful online behaviour of cutting off your internet access. This may mean foregoing your mobile device for a period of time or part of the day (perhaps leaving your phone or tablet at home when you go to work, or vice versa); it may mean closing down accounts for particular websites. It may mean shutting off your internet access at certain times, such as overnight, whether by installing timers or dedicated software (search the web for the best options for your make of router), or by manually switching off the router.

3. *Replace one habit with another.* Fasting from connectivity (or anything) has a purpose. The intention is not simply to leave a vacuum that you unthinkingly fill, possibly with something equally harmful. Instead, look for ways of using the time and extra energy to do something productive, whether that is praying and reading the Bible, getting some exercise, meeting with friends or something else. Make sure there is something involved that provides a reward of some sort, just as there is typically a 'reward' that incentivises harmful actions. Don't expect to establish a new habit overnight: start small and build up steadily.

4. *Learn to recognise triggers.* Although many of these vices are habitual and compulsive, they will often have a trigger – typically stress, boredom or tiredness, which may be the reason we seek escapism online more

---

119 Which I do not endorse.

generally. Learning to recognise triggers is an important step in addressing harmful habits and gives you an early warning signal to step away and try something else.

5. *Inform yourself.* More positively, use the web and social media to learn the truth about issues that motivate you. These might concern human rights abuses, news of events in countries that are typically not reported by mainstream media, developments in technology or other areas that are overlooked or misunderstood – there is no substitute for grassroots opinion. Mainstream news is always filtered through the political affiliation of the media organisation, and often by the interests, capabilities and even time available for the reporter. Remember the rule from Proverbs 18:17, 'In a lawsuit the first to speak seems right, until someone comes forward and cross-examines.'

6. *Use what influence you have.* Your social media feeds may be a series of pictures of other people's meals and captioned cats, but there's no question that social networking is an excellent way to inform yourself and other people about events of significance. If you can promote awareness and engagement for important issues, do so.

CONCLUSION

The last two decades have seen unprecedented changes in the way we communicate. Back in the mid-90s, the easiest way to talk to someone at a distance was to pick up the phone – even write a letter, if you had the inclination. Those were really the only options, unless both of you happened to be early adopters who had hooked your computer up to the phone network to set up email accounts or use chatrooms.

Since then, the number of options has dramatically increased. There's email, of course, but although that's now used extensively (with over 200 billion sent per day),[120] people are increasingly turning to other forms of communication that are even faster – text messages, mobile instant messaging and social networking. Whilst phone calls are one-to-one[121] and emails are one-to-one or one-to-many, social networking is many-to-many – you can post something that will be seen by hundreds or thousands of people, any of whom can reply. This means the volume of messages we receive or to which we are exposed has increased exponentially.

The ease with which we can communicate with each other is just one of the far-reaching changes the information revolution has brought. These technologies are not in themselves good, or bad, or neutral – but their specific applications will necessarily have

---

120 http://www.radicati.com/wp/wp-content/uploads/2015/02/Email-Statistics-Report-2015-2019-Executive-Summary.pdf
121 Voice-only conference calls are generally still awkward and expensive, and video calling has grown in popularity thanks to applications like Skype and FaceTime.

moral, relational and spiritual impacts, just as the application and implications of ironworking, the cotton gin, encryption or nuclear technology can be positive or negative.

BEFORE BABEL

At its best, there is something enormously liberating about communications technology. The ability to connect with other people, wherever they are around the world – and, thanks to translation software, sometimes even regardless of language – is almost pre-Babellian. It has the capacity to draw us closer together by emphasising our shared humanity over any differences of nationality or accidents of geography. Social media has made the world a smaller place and helped many people to re-establish the idea of community, albeit in redefined form. It serves as a reminder at the human level of the spiritual principle Paul states in Galatians 3:28, regardless of whether those with whom we communicate are Christians. 'There is neither Jew nor Gentile, neither slave nor free, nor is there male and female, for you are all one in Christ Jesus.'

The ability to connect with others can have profound consequences for our spiritual freedom, and – critically – for the freedom of those with whom we are in relationship. Social media-based church communities are a good example of this. It also has implications for political freedoms. Decentralisation of power is a key principle in the Bible, something God built into the Israelites' structures of government and justice after their experiences as slaves under Pharaoh in Egypt. This is important because the nature of a country's government plays a key role in guaranteeing its citizens' religious freedoms, or otherwise – China being an obvious example.

On another level, we have never been more informed as consumers. We are able to research every purchase and every significant decision we make online, reading reviews from other customers about products, services and companies from books to mortgage deals and insurers. We no longer have to believe what we are told by the vendors; the web brings transparency and accountability in commerce and finance as well as politics. We can be better stewards of the financial resources God has given us, thereby reducing debt, having more money to give to charity, and more to spend on family and other priorities. In theory, then, communications technologies can emphasise our shared humanity and bring us closer to God.

The problem is that, as the saying goes, 'In theory, theory and practice are the same. In practice, they're not.' Humans are social animals. Communicating is fundamental to who we are. God created us for relationship, both with him and with each other. But we are also fallen creatures, made in the image of God but flawed and predisposed to making mistakes that damage relationships – in fact, the implication of Matthew 22:34–40 is that sin *is* anything that damages one or other relationship, a failure to love God and love neighbour. And so the same technologies that allow us to be better communicators, live in better relationship with each other – more direct and open, more just, better informed, *more human* – also bring the opportunity to hamstring ourselves and make us *less human*, less perfect reflections of the image of the Creator.

Thanks to our fallen nature, we have an innate tendency to make bad decisions. There is always a slight tug towards options that are more selfish, like a supermarket trolley that won't steer straight and insists on drifting off course unless you consciously take the effort to keep it on the straight and narrow.

So, whilst there is much that is positive about our adoption of communications technologies, when we use them uncritically our 'default-to-negative' trait means the benefits are overlaid with behaviours that harm our relationships, reducing or cancelling out their advantages. We are more connected than ever before. This could make us better people – but it doesn't always. That takes discernment and a deliberate effort to use them well.

'I WILL NOT BE MASTERED'

Technology is power, and that power plays out in the myriad different relationships of which we are a part. We are fallen beings, but we are also relational and spiritual beings (the relational being an integral part of the spiritual). If God is lord over all of our lives, then there is nothing we do that does not have some kind of spiritual implications, strange as that may seem.

Jesus calls for our full allegiance: that we submit every part of our lives to him and there is nothing that we hold back. And this is the fundamental question when it comes to the web, smartphones and social media. Technology is always, inherently about power. It gives all of us the ability to do things we would not otherwise have been able to do. Do we take up that power ourselves, using it in ways that are aligned with the ideals of God's kingdom, or do we let others take it up and use it against us by setting the tone for our lives – making us passive consumers of values that are not our own and do not reflect God's will? That is the danger here and the theme we have explored throughout this book: '"I have the right to do anything" – but I will not be mastered by anything' (1 Corinthians 6:12).

Thus using this or any technology in a way that strengthens and aligns with our faith means engaging with it deliberately, placing boundaries around it and ensuring that it does not cross the line from being a servant to a master. That might mean not being sucked in by the never-ending flood of content that threatens constant distraction, undermining our ability to focus and, implicitly, reducing our capacity to relate to each other – in the most basic terms, to love. It might mean recognising that 'time is the currency of relationships', and that when we allow work to encroach into other areas of life then there are inevitably winners and losers. (Given that there are only twenty-four hours a day, our use of time on one thing will always be at the expense of something else. This isn't to say that work or other online relationships aren't valid, only that it is easy unintentionally to spend time on one task and wish, retrospectively, that we had not – time has a surprising way of being eaten up without us noticing until it's too late.) It might mean acknowledging that the anonymity of the web means we can edit our personality online, or even create a new one, but that this has implications for our character and integrity.

Then, of course, there is the power of consumerism, an ideology that pervades our culture and is arguably its dominant value system. The ability to choose anything and everything we want, from goods and services to ideas and beliefs, and to change our minds at will and shape our lives around ourselves, raises questions about what we truly value. In a world of such fluidity, where everything is subject to change according to what suits us best, what place is there for love, faithfulness and stability? What does it mean to have our identity in Christ, when consumerism tells us that who we are is up for grabs on a daily basis?

The extent to which we willingly submit to forces that would seek to control us is also raised by issues of privacy and surveillance. This includes not only the governments (domestic and foreign) who collect personal data about us, but corporations that seek to gather information in order to influence our spending habits.

Ultimately, the power we are granted through our use of communications technology comes down to freedom and responsibility. God gave us free will, which includes the ability to make bad choices as well as good ones. The web, smartphones and social media, like any technologies, expand the range and impact of the choices we can make – and the choices that others make that affect us. It is the same with the gospel. The gospel gives us freedom: freedom from condemnation, freedom from the Law, freedom from the enslaving habits of the world. But this freedom also comes with responsibility, because we have the freedom to walk away from God as well as follow him. As Paul writes, we are free to commit ourselves to Godly living:

You, my brothers and sisters, were called to be free. But do not use your freedom to indulge the flesh; rather, serve one another humbly in love. For the entire law is fulfilled in keeping this one command: 'Love your neighbour as yourself.' If you bite and devour each other, watch out or you will be destroyed by each other.

GALATIANS 5:13–15

DIGITALLY REMASTERED

'Do you not know that wrongdoers will not inherit the kingdom of God?' writes Paul, before listing a series of the Corinthians' favourite sins. 'And that is what some of you were. But you were washed, you were sanctified, you were justified in the name of the Lord Jesus Christ and by the Spirit of our God' (1 Corinthians 6:9, 11).

Our sanctification may be a one-off event, something that occurs at the point of conversion, but remaining in step with God's will is an ongoing process that will last the rest of our lives. Jesus alludes to this when he washes the disciples' feet before the Last Supper.

He came to Simon Peter, who said to him, 'LORD, are you going to wash my feet?' Jesus replied, 'You do not realise now what I am doing, but later you will understand.' 'No,' said Peter, 'you shall never wash my feet.' Jesus answered, 'Unless I wash you, you have no part with me.'

'Then, LORD,' Simon Peter replied, 'not just my feet but my hands and my head as well!' Jesus answered, 'Those who have had a bath need only to wash their feet; their whole body is clean.'

JOHN 13:6–10

This slightly cryptic exchange has far greater significance than solely for personal hygiene.[122] It refers to the Christian's routine 'maintenance' of seeking God's forgiveness. 'The true believer is thus washed when he receives Christ for his salvation. See then what ought to be the daily care of those who through grace are in a justified state, and that is, to wash their feet; to cleanse themselves from daily guilt, and to watch against everything defiling.'[123]

We have been sanctified and freed, but this does not mean we are immune to the daily temptations posed by our continued existence in a fallen world. In the case of communications technologies, the temptations are proportional to the attractions. There is the danger that, like Adam and Eve in the Garden of Eden, we allow ourselves to be mastered by an idea that seems fantastic in principle but has unforeseen downsides.

And so our use of technology can bring us closer to God, and closer to each other. Or it can drive us further away. The difference is a matter of discernment. The challenge for us is not to be mastered by them, or by anything, but daily to be re-Mastered to walk more closely with God.

Guy Brandon, Jubilee Centre, June 2016

---

122 Important though personal hygiene is.
123 *Matthew Henry's Concise Commentary.*